POSTCARD

LAURENCE KING

Published in 2008 by
Laurence King Publishing Ltd
361-373 City Road
London EC1V 1LR
email: enquiries@laurenceking.co.uk
www.laurenceking.co.uk

A catalogue record for this book
is available from the British Library.

ISBN: 978-185669-569-5

Words and image selection:
Agathe Jacquillat and
Tomi Vollauschek at FL@33

Cover images:
Top: 'Peter Pan' © Jan von Holleben
Bottom: © Emily Forgot

Project editor: Gaynor Sermon
Copyeditor: Jenny Doubt

Book design:
FL@33
www.flat33.com

Printed in China

POSTCARD

Agathe Jacquillat and Tomi Vollauschek at FL@33

Laurence King Publishing

6 INTRODUCTION

INTRO

Dedication:
For Cosmo and Stanley

hen we had the initial idea to
ompile a book on contemporary
ostcards we didn't quite realize
ow many fantastic cards by other
tists we had actually been
athering over the last few years,
nd quite how many examples of
xciting contemporary postcards
e already out there. As it turned
ut, many other artists and
esigners appear to have the
ame hunter and gatherer gene,
nd have been obsessively
ollecting postcards as well! It
d not therefore come as a big
rprise when we received an
verwhelming number of postcard
bmissions from around the world
r inclusion in this book, from
e great to the experimental,
omplete with tips and further
commendations.

uring our research we learned
at Deltiology – the collecting
nd study of postcards – is
pparently one of the most
opular hobbies in the world. But
efore we talk about today's age
instant messaging, here is a very
ief summary of a few milestones
the relatively short – though truly
ernational – history of the
ostcard. The first genuine
ostcard originated in Austria in
69 and became available for
e in what was then the Austro-
ungarian Empire. That first
ostcard consisted of a blank
rd with a pre-printed stamp. This
w, brief form of correspondence
oved so popular that many
untries followed suit within a
w years. England's Post Office
ued the equivalent British version
1870.

Boosted by the International
Exhibition in Paris in 1889, picture
postcards became increasingly
popular and widely available
around the world. Interestingly,
back then the law did not permit
users of any country to write on
the address side of a postcard.
Cards thus had little designated
blank spaces for short messages
on the picture side of the
postcard. In 1902, England was
the first country to allow 'divided
back' cards, which meant that
addresses and messages could
be written on the same side of the
postcard. This enabled the front
of the card to be dedicated to
featuring an artwork or picture.
By 1907 'divided back' cards
were permitted in many other
countries, including France,
Germany and the USA. The golden
age of postcards had well and
truly begun.

Since the boom of the *Having
a lovely time – wish you were
here* picture postcard, the world
has changed, and 'instant'
correspondence has become the
priority. But despite the availability
of free e-cards, emails, sms/texts
and media messages, the humble
postcard remains a thriving
medium. Artists, designers,
illustrators and photographers
continue to explore the endless
possibilities of this small canvas.

This book features some
extraordinary examples of
contemporary postcards and
showcases just how versatile
this artform is. Postcards – and
similarly posters, T-shirts and button
badges – can be inexpensively
produced, indicating that they will
remain popular for some time to
come, be it as handmade mail art,
one-off mixed-media artworks,
collectors and limited-edition
pieces or for purely commercial
marketing means such as
promotions and advertising.

Many innovative postcards
and postcard-related projects
presented in this book push the
boundaries of the traditional uses
of the postcard. Examples include
cards that are edible, animated
(lenticular), musical, transformable
(into jewellery), templates for
stencil-spray art and even a
postcard that (once planted)
grows into a plant. Selected
postcards are witty, humorous and
beautiful. Although some of the
projects contained within these
pages could have been classified
according to many of the book's
five chapters, we have attempted
to make clear delineations
between B.I.O. (By Invitation Only),
Specials, Postcards, Books and Sets
and Ongoing Projects.

We hope you find this selection
of works by emerging and
established talents, companies
and artistic institutions as inspiring
as we do.

Agathe Jacquillat and
Tomi Vollauschek, FL@33

B.I.O.
(BY INVITATION ONLY)

The 20 designs featured in this chapter are also included with the book as free postcards for you to collect, display or send. We invited some of the world's leading designers, artists and image-makers to contribute previously unpublished work or to design a postcard especially for the book.

0.11

Return to sender

Daniel Eatock

eatock.com

United Kingdom

London-based Daniel Eatock's artwork engages in a variety of themes, including the connection between image and language, punch lines, miscommunication, subversion, seriality, discovery and invention. His conceptual art invites reductive, logical and objective interpretations from viewers. One of Eatock's most noteworthy artistic fascinations is with the connection between the start and end points of a hand-drawn circle.

aving lived in Rwanda, the United Arab Emirates and Indonesia, and
udied in London and Berlin, Julia Schonlau settled in her native Germany
here she set up her Berlin-based company, Juju's Delivery, in 2003. Her
stinct illustration style quickly helped her to gain an international
putation, and a limited edition showcase book of her work *The Dead,*
e Damned and the Children of the Revolution was published in 2005 by
ojo Editions (Barcelona). Schonlau's body of work for clients such as MTV,
hart and Graniph includes album covers, posters, T-shirts, murals, cars
nd skateboards – to name just a few.

Juju's Delivery

Design: Julia Schonlau

jujus-delivery.com

Germany

Jeremyville

jeremyville.com

Australia and USA

Jeremyville is an artist, product designer and animator who divides his time between his studios in Sydney and New York City. Publications of his work include *Vinyl Will Kill*, the world's first book on designer toys, and a book on collaborative projects entitled *Jeremyville Sessions*. Jeremyville also initiated the 'sketchel' – a custom art satchel project whose 500 collaborators include artists such as Beck and Geneviève Gauckler. Among his clients are Converse, Coca Cola, MTV and 55 DSL.

Above: *'This is about my collective memories of many saturdays spent in Soho, New York. Most saturdays involve a lunch at Cafe Gitane in Nolita, coffee from Dean and Deluca, hanging out at the Apple Store, a trip further downtown to get some roasted nuts from Cafe Bazzini in Tribeca then a drink at The Mercer Hotel. This is sort of a postcard to myself.'*

cien and Klor have been graffiti artists since 1989. After discovering eville Brody's work on typography, they changed their style and troduced graphic art as an extension to their graffiti writing. 123Klan ere the first artists to blend graffiti writing and graphic art on the web, sing the internet not just as an exhibition space but also as a new reative medium. For these trailblazers, graffiti writing and graphic art e closely linked and, 'style is the message'. Their monograph was ublished in 2004 and an updated edition was released in 2007 as part the design&designer series by French publisher Pyramyd Editions. ormerly based in France, they now live in Canada.

123Klan

Design: Klor and Scien

123klan.com

Canada

Geneviève Gauckler

g2works.com

France

Geneviève Gauckler graduated from the ENSAD (Ecole Nationale Supérieure des Arts Décoratifs) in 1991 in Paris, where she lives and works. Gauckler's trademark style fuses photography with vector graphics, and much of her work toys with the relationship between people and reality; the 'mega-silly' and lovable characters that appear in her art are often blended into everyday life scenes. Three books have been published about Gauckler's work: by Gas Book in Japan and by Pyramyd in France. Geneviève has also been a member of the experimental video collective Pleix since 2001. Her clients include Renault, Bourjois, Coca-Cola, Lane Crawford and Skype.

...LOVE IS ALL...

Working in art, graphic design and illustration, Catalina Estrada creates usive worlds replete with colour, nature and enchanting characters. resented as a fresh and new design talent by *Communication Arts* and *Computer Arts* magazines, her work has also been featured by Die estalten Verlag, *Swindle*, DPI, Ppaper and *Graphic Magazine*. Some of er clients include: Paul Smith, Coca-Cola, Custo-Barcelona, Salomon, onda, Nike and Chronicle Books.

Catalina Estrada

catalinaestrada.com

Spain

Marion Deuchars

mariondeuchars.com

United Kingdom

Marion Deuchars studied Illustration and Printmaking at Duncan of Jordanstone College of Art before obtaining her MA from the Royal College of Art in 1989. Along with other RCA students, she founded the multi-disciplinary art and design studio in North London that she continues to work from. Deuchars has also worked with major design and advertising agencies worldwide. The artwork featured on the postcard above was created in 2006 and is taken from her sketchbooks. It was produced in response to current news events that Deuchars was covering for *The Guardian*, who later published the illustrations. Her clients include Ford France, Royal Mail, Virgin, Marks & Spencer, Formula One, D&AD, Penguin books, Aiko Italy, Harrods and *Esquire NY*.

...ellovon is run by London-based illustrator Von. His work is heavily ...fluenced by music, fashion and design, and executed with a seamless ...end of traditional and digital mark-making techniques. The resulting ...stration style has both an insightful and ethereal quality. Since ...tablishing Hellovon in 2006, Von's work has been exhibited internationally ...the London Design Museum, Cosh, Espeis, Exposure, Soma, Triple 5 Soul ...d Stolen Space galleries. He has also built a client list that includes 4AD, ...gilvy and Mather, Non-Format, *Dazed & Confused*, *Wallpaper*, *The New ...rk Times* and *The Guardian*.

Hellovon

Design: Von

hellovon.com

United Kingdom

eBoy

eBoy.com

Germany

Berlin-based eBoy was founded in 1998 when Steffen Sauerteig, Svend Smital and Kai Vermehr acquired the eBoy.com domain. With no printing and low production costs, and the ability to send data to the most distant reaches of the globe in seconds, eBoy is designed to embrace the new possibilities of the emerging digital world. Since artwork is designed specifically for the screen, eBoy emphasises the use of pixels, ensuring both creative control over their work as well as an innovative approach. Uniquely, eBoy only features freestyle work on its website. Clients such as MTV.com, SAP, Adidas and many more have hired eBoy, and in doing so, have propelled the so-called 'pixel style' all over the world. *Hello*, a book celebrating their work, was published in 2002 by Laurence King.

dual Swiss and British nationality, Gregory Gilbert-Lodge is based in
rich, Switzerland. He is an award-winning illustrator, working mainly
m an editorial client-base. Until 2005 he was a member of Silex – a
up of seven artists and illustrators – whose book *Silex – My Way* was
blished in 2000 by Die Gestalten Verlag. Gilbert-Lodge's work has
en exhibited internationally and has also been published in numerous
agazines and books. His latest high-profile publication *Two Faced* (2007)
atures beautiful and striking portraits. *The Kiss* (above) is the author's
erpretation of the *'two girls (Naomi Watts and Laura Elena Harring)
sing each other in David Lynch's film* Mulholland Drive.*'*

Gregory Gilbert-Lodge

gilbert-lodge.com

Switzerland

Supermundane

supermundane.com

United Kingdom

Supermundane is part of a new era of artists with multi-disciplinary backgrounds. Having worked in graphic design for over 12 years, he has been variously known as an art director, typographer, illustrator, graphic artist and writer. His typography on *Sleaze* magazine and the art directio and design of *Good For Nothing* magazine took his pared down, hand produced aesthetic to a wider audience. He has had work published an exhibited worldwide and was picked as one of 25 emerging design taler in 2004 by the New York magazine *Step (Inside Design)*. Supermundane's several solo exhibitions depict utopian worlds and beasts displaying hop melancholy and beauty. He has produced work for Playstation, Orange, Hoegaarden, Colette, Juliet Lewis and many more.

I LIKE IT HERE

A.B.

thony Burrill studied Graphic Design at Leeds Polytechnic before
mpleting his MA at the Royal College of Art, London. He works as
reelance designer, producing print, moving image and interactive
signs based on direct communication with viewers. Humour often plays
central role in his artworks. His projects have included poster campaigns
London Underground, DIESEL, Hans Brinker Budget Hotel, Playstation,
e and interactive web-based projects for Kraftwerk and Air. Burrill lives
d works on the Isle of Oxney, Kent.

Anthony Burrill

anthonyburrill.com

United Kingdom

Tabas

Design: Cédric Malo

tabas.fr

France

An arts and calligraphy enthusiast, Cédric Malo has been working as a graphic designer since 1996. After starting out alongside members of the Tous des K collective, in 2000 he set up his own studio, Tabas, in Marseille and has undertaken commissions for music labels (including Sony Music and Wagram) and public institutions (such as the City of Marseille and the regional tourist board). Malo uses a craft-like approach to his personal work, which includes paintings on cardboard, photography and rag doll. His colourful and playful designs are, by virtue of their simplicity, accessible to a wide audience. His first monograph was published in 2004 as part of the design&designer series by Pyramyd Editions.

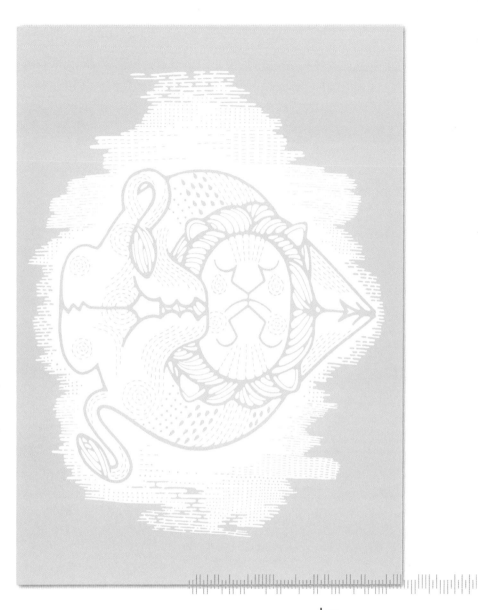

sign and art collective Rinzen is best known for the collaborative
proach of its five members, forming as a result of their pioneering visual
d audio remix project, RMX. In 2001 the group invited more than 30
ernational participants to sequentially rework digital art, and this
proach has now become a common method of collaboration among
aphic designers and illustrators. Rinzen's work, created both individually
d as a collective, covers a wide range of styles and techniques, often
aturing utopian alternate realities, bold, geometric designs or intricate,
nd drawn studies. Members of the group are based in Berlin, Brisbane,
lbourne and New York. This postcard is entitled *Solar Powered*.

Rinzen

Design: Adrian Clifford

rinzen.com

Australia

Andrzej Klimowski

klimowski.com

United Kingdom

Born to Polish parents in London in 1949, Andrzej Klimowski trained at the Saint Martin's School of Art before studying at the Academy of Fine Art and working professionally in Warsaw. From the late 1970s Klimowski has designed posters, book jackets, illustrations, TV graphics and animations, which all delineate a strong Polish School influence. Also a Professor in Illustration at the Royal College of Art, London, his broader body of work extends to short films, illustrations and books. His work has recently been the subject of a retrospective at London's Theatre Museum. *'Camera'* (above), is made from gouache on paper, and is previously unpublished

Greetings from helvetica

fantastic
famous
font

witness
the
boldness

explore
tight
kerning

visit
the
caps

leave
serifs
behind

rgo Tloupas is the co-founder and creative director of *Intersection* agazine. He divides his time between his native Paris and London, here *Intersection* is based. Tloupas also works as a freelance designer d art director for various fashion, art, music and automobile clients. *ent to helvetica and all I got was this lousy set of characters*, is cribed on the back of this postcard (above), which was designed pecially for this book.

Yorgo Tloupas

intersectionmagazine.com

yorgo.co.uk

France and United Kingdom

Mark Adams

markadamsimages.com

United Kingdom

Mark Adams is a freelance photographic artist who was born in Birmingham in 1971. In 2001 he received a MA in Communication Art and Design from the Royal College of Art. When he temporarily moved to California in 2002 to teach photography in San Francisco, the focus of Adams' work shifted to include predominantly street and colour landscape photography. He moved back to the UK in 2007 and is based in Manchester, teaching Visual Communication at Doncester College. Exhibits of his work have been mounted in the United States and England and he is represented by Millennium Images. *Land Development Site #2, Galveston, Texas, USA* is featured above.

London by night

sabeth Lecourt was born in France in 1972. She moved to the United
ngdom in 1992 and obtained her MA from London's Royal College of Art
2001. She exhibits both in Europe and the United States. Lecourt's art
cuses on disclosure, using life events in works ranging from storytelling,
awing, installation, painting, embroidered handkerchiefs and sculpture.
er notable *Les Robes Géographiques* series includes maps which form
othes and garments.

Elisabeth Lecourt

elisabethlecourt.com

United Kingdom

PMT 23: no show

Vaughan Oliver at v23

v-23.co.uk

United Kingdom

Independent record label 4AD's look was designed by Vaughan in 1980 and has been maintained for over 25 years. Supported by Chris Bigg since 1988, v23 was formed in 1998 when Bigg and Vaughan formalized their partnership. Clients include: 4AD, V&A Publishing, L'Oreal, Central Saint Martin's, Coco de Mer, Microsoft, Sony, Harrods, Alberto Aspesi, John Galliano and Young Vic Theatre.

PMT 23 artwork (above), was created using a photo mechanical transfer camera, the repro cameras traditionally used to copy artworks. According to Vaughan, *'its process could, however, be subverted for more creative use. This is an image of the baseboard of the camera, or self-portrait – or a picture of nothing. For me, its drama is very arresting!'*

@33 is a multi-disciplinary visual communication studio based in London. founders Agathe (French) and Tomi (Austrian from Germany) met at e Royal College of Art in 1999 and set up FL@33 after graduating in 2001. e studio's clients include Sacla, BBC, MTV Networks, Royal Festival Hall, roupe Galeries Lafayette and Friends of the Earth. They launched ereohype.com, a graphic art and fashion boutique, in 2004 and have leased independent projects such as the award-winning *trans-form* agazine and the sound collection bzzzpeek.com. A FL@33 monograph as published in 2005 as part of the design&designer book series by ramyd Editions. *Please Meet our Friendly Postman* is featured above.

FL@33

Design: Agathe Jacquillat

and Tomi Vollauschek

flat33.com

United Kingdom

SPECIALS

Postcards and postcard-related
projects in this chapter push the
boundaries of the traditional
postcard format, including musical
and animated cards, cards that can
be eaten, transformed into items
such as jewellery, used as templates
for stencil-spray art and even a
postcard that grows when planted.

0.33

Johnson Banks

Design: Michael Johnson

johnsonbanks.co.uk

United Kingdom

London's V&A Museum organize an annual *Village Fête* fair, offering an eclectic variety of games and products from 30 of the most creative individuals working in the UK. When asked to mount a stall at the fête, Johnson Banks took his influence from the post office. An alphabet of die-cut postcards was the result. The Send a Letter series consists of 26 multi-coloured die-cut, letter-shaped postcards. Each card is two-colour with silver foil blocking on the reverse. Initially designed in 2005, they were reprinted on brighter, thicker paper in a strictly-limited 2007 edition.

Send a letter

from the
johnson banks
post office

Pun post
from the
johnson banks
post office

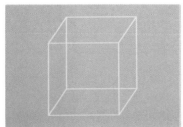

johnsonbanks.co.uk

United Kingdom

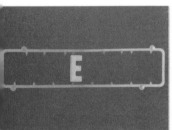
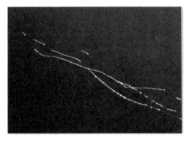

The Pun Post series was developed in 2005 by Johnson Banks. Each card in the series illustrates a groan-inducing post-related pun. Recycled postcards based on found scraps therefore became *Junk Mail*. Bubble wrap made logical *Airmail*. And God seemed the most appropriate illustration for *Address Unknown*. Many of the cards are also finished by hand. Thus hundreds of copies of *Drop Me a Line* had to be individually stitched. Each *Hot Mail* is hand burnt, while all *Postal Strike* cards have been struck with a match. Shown here are just a few examples of the 33 cards that were submitted.

Opposite: *Air Mail, Drop Me a Line, Hot Mail, Post Card, Registered Post, Post It, Mail Order, Fly Post.*

Left: *Postal Strike, Post Box, Direct Mail, Post Mark, E mail, Scratch Card, Goal Post, French Letters, Direct Mail, Address Unknown.*

April-Mediengruppe

Design: Karin Kloubert

april-mg.de

Germany

The idea behind the edible gingerbread postcard *Against X-mas Panic* was first conceived in December 2004 for a design auction at the Notting Hill Arts Club in London. Berlin-based Karin Kloubert developed her idea in 2005, and produced a limited edition of 250 handmade copies – with coloured icing sugar. All postcards feature the same slogan, illustrated with varying colours and typefaces. Plastic packaging was added to protect the gingerbread postcards as they travelled to deliver their Christmas greetings.

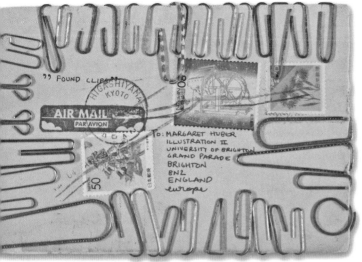

Recent graduate of the Royal College of Art, Riitta Ikonen created the project *Mail Art – Location, Vocation, Vacation* in 2004. During her journeys to Japan, her native Finland, Spain, Russia and England, Ikonen sent 70 A6-sized cards to Margaret Huber, her former tutor at the University of Brighton. Cards created from hair, fish, a sachet of white powder, a piece of broken record, and other collected materials, were sent both as a record of experiences from around the world – and also to test the postal system. Only three cards failed to reach their final destination.

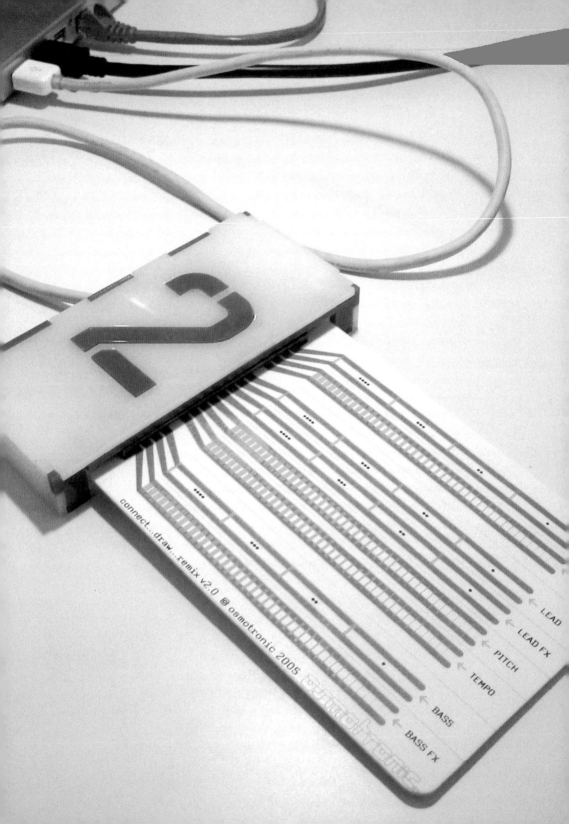

connect...draw...remix v2.0 @ osmotronic 2005

LEAD
LEAD FX
PITCH
TEMPO
BASS
BASS FX

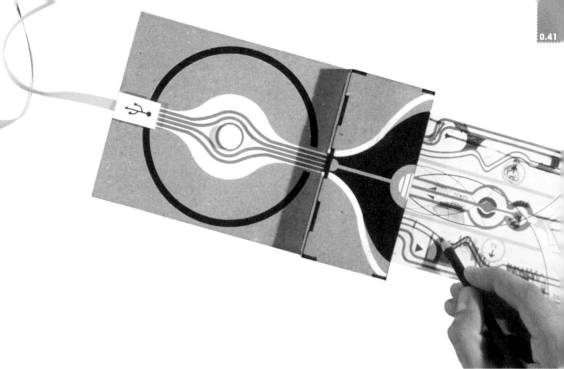

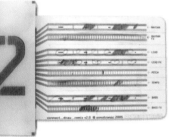

Osmotronic

Design: Matthew Falla

matthewfalla.com

United Kingdom

London-based designer Matthew Falla created *Connect... Draw... Remix* (previously known as *CD Sequencer*) in 2005 and fine-tuned the acoustic postcard project in 2007. Complete with cardboard packaging, an enhanced audio CD and a set of printed postcards, this innovative new concept for interactive CD packaging uses conductive ink which allows consumers to adapt the accompanying CD tracks by manipulating the packaging with computer software and a simple pencil. Responding to the decline in sales of physical music formats, *Connect... Draw... Remix* is an attempt to bolster sales of physical musical formats.

How to use *Connect... Draw...* : First connect the box to your PC using a USB cable. Take one of the supplied printed postcards that come with the CD and slot it into the side of the box. Finally take a pencil and start drawing on the cards to remix the tunes.

How to *Remix*: As soon as you make a pencil mark, elements of the track begin to play: bass lines, melodies and rhythm tracks, along with effects such as tempo and pitch. If you make a mistake or want to revert to a previous version, 'undo' by using a standard pencil eraser. Once happy with a mix, remove the card and save it for later. The remix is 'stored' on the postcard until the next time it is inserted into the box, when it will playback.

Iceberg

Art Direction: Simona Castellani

Design: Chris Rocchegiani

Client: Rondinella

iceberg.it

Italy

Italian agency Iceberg created this Christmas card for children's footware manufacturer Rondinella (Swallow). Each card contains shapes that, once pulled out and fitted together, become a stylized swallow, the logo of the company. A small gift to celebrate Christmas – and the company's 70th anniversary.

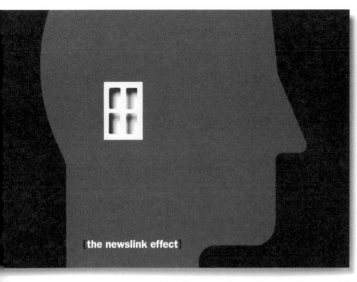

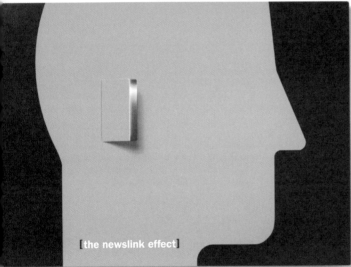

Creative Direction: Gareth Howat,

David Kimpton and Jim Sutherland

Design: Gareth Howat

Client: Newslink

hat-trickdesign.co.uk

United Kingdom

Newslink is a network advertising media space within news bulletins on commercial radio stations. Previously untapped by advertisers, Newslink drew on research that shows that listeners are most receptive when they listen (attentively) to the news. Newslink chose to advertise this opportunity to media buyers via Hat-trick-produced postcards, which were sent weekly by direct mail. The cards illustrate a series of key product values in a simple graphic style, demonstrating Newslink's ability to cut through media proliferation.

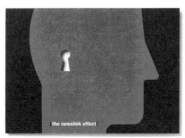

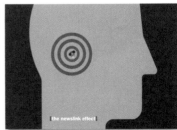

Hat-trick

Creative Direction: Gareth Howat,

David Kimpton and Jim Sutherland

Design: Ben Christie

Client: Bankside 123

hat-trickdesign.co.uk

United Kingdom

Land Securities is Europe's largest property development company, with an £8 billion (US $16 billion) portfolio. Its London programme, Capital Commitment, needed a direct mail piece to help market its latest three-building Bankside development. Adapting the '1, 2, 3' theme established throughout the development campaign, a three-stage lenticular map entitled *Location, Location, Location* was created by London-based design consultancy Hat-trick. When tilted at different angles, the map variously reveals transport links, sites of interest and a road map.

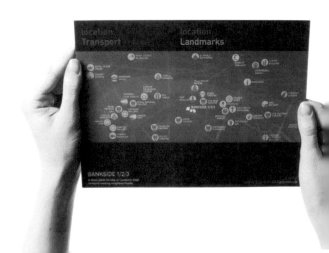

Nicole Jacek

Client: MVP

nicolejacek@aol.com

Germany

Every second year a traditional *Ochsenfest* (ox festival) takes place in Ludwigsburg, Germany. Over the years the festival has developed from a feast of barbecued ox into a music festival renowned for its live rock, jazz and traditional German music. Having designed the original logo – a silhouette of an ox – for the festival, Nicole Jacek decided to revisit the logo in light of the festival's new focus. The new logo creates an animation in six steps, inviting a visualization of the festival's metamorphosis. By slowly moving the postcard, the original logo morphs into an ox whose head twists upward into the shape of an electric guitar.

WITH COMPLIMENTS

TEL 03 6277 3360/61   FAX 03 6277 3362
MOBILE 080 3206 7739   LARS@LESSRAIN.COM
WWW.LESSRAIN.CO.JP

LESS RAIN
154-0001
東京都世田谷区池尻 2-4-5
IID 201-B

201-B IID 2-4-5 IKEJIRI
SETAGAYA-KU
154-0001 TOKYO
JAPAN

Lars Eberle
founder
ラース　エーベルレ

TEL 03 6277 3360/61   FAX 03 6277 3362
MOBILE 080 1159 9156   PATRICK@LESSRAIN.COM
WWW.LESSRAIN.CO.JP

LESS RAIN
154-0001
東京都世田谷区池尻 2-4-5
IID 201-B

201-B IID 2-4-5 IKEJIRI
SETAGAYA-KU
154-0001 TOKYO
JAPAN

Patrick Juchli
interactive director
パトリック　ユフリ

TEL 03 6277 3360/61   FAX 03 6277 3362
MOBILE 090 8506 0132   SHIHO@LESSRAIN.COM
WWW.LESSRAIN.CO.JP

LESS RAIN
154-0001
東京都世田谷区池尻 2-4-5
IID 201-B

201-B IID 2-4-5 IKEJIRI
SETAGAYA-KU
154-0001 TOKYO
JAPAN

Shiho Tremmel
chief producer
トレメル 志保

Carsten Schneid
designer, director

Less Rain, Tokyo

Design: Lars Eberle

Photography: Lars Eberle and

Sonia Mueller

lessrain.com

Japan

Design agency Less Rain was founded in 1997 in London, and has offices in Berlin and Tokyo. Co-founder and creative director Lars Eberle heads the Tokyo office. The websites that they build are 'small worlds' – immersive environments with a consistent visual and interactive element. The visual identity for their Tokyo office is based on postcards designed as holiday snapshots, inviting people not only to negotiate travel in cyberspace with Less Rain, but also to have their very own 'small world' custom built.

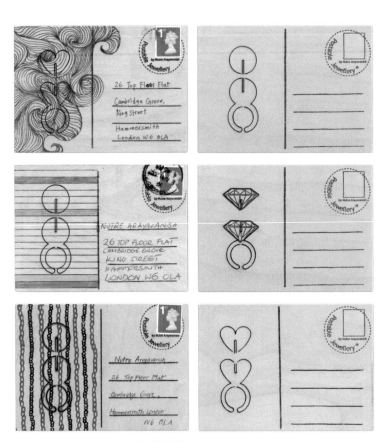

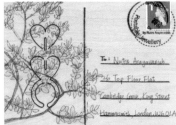

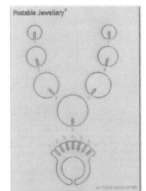

nutrejeweller.com

United Kingdom

Nutre Arayavanish graduated from the Royal College of Art, London in 2007. Her unique jewellery postcards are designed to fit through a letterbox, and recipients can assemble flat-packed rings by slotting together individual components. Arayavanish developed this format to suggest that the actual journey from sender to receiver is a crucial part of communicating: *'Letters, postcards or greeting cards always bear the evidence of the journey: marks, stamps, stains or scratches on them.'*

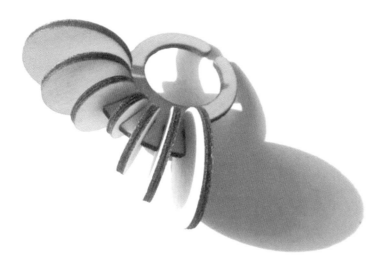

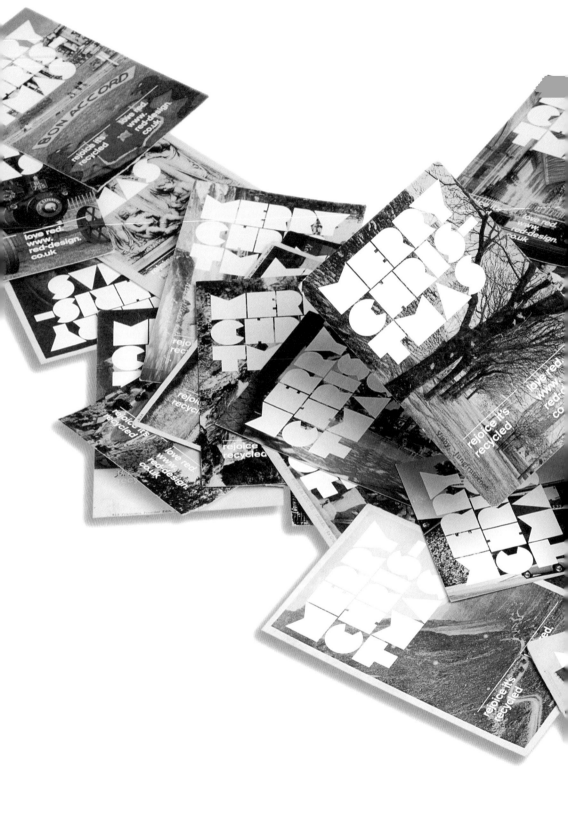

red-design.co.uk

United Kingdom

Brighton-based Red Design created the project *Rejoice it's Recycled* in 2006. In this series, the artists use recycled postcards as unique canvases for screenprinted Season's greetings.

Köln a. Rh.

Universität

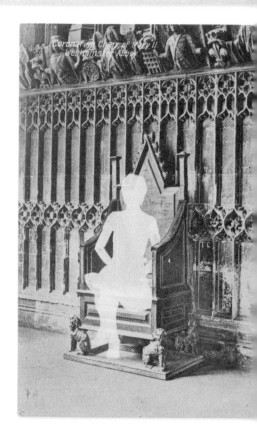

Coronation Chair of Mary II
Westminster Abbey

CÆSAR'S TOWER, WARWICK CASTLE   PHOTO. J. J. WARD, COVENTRY

Danielle Palmstrom

danielle.palmstrom@gmail.com

USA

The Travel series is a set of personal postcards by Danielle Palmstrom. Using photography, found postcards and silkscreening, Palmstrom incorporates herself into the various antiquated settings that her cards display by imposing her likeness onto older, worn images. Danielle graduated with a BFA in Graphic Design from Rhode Island School of Design (RISD) in 2006. She lives and works in New York City.

The Fine Arts Publishing Co., Ltd., London.

SHAKESPEARE'S BIRTHPLACE: THE BIRTH ROOM.

DO NOT

DISTURB

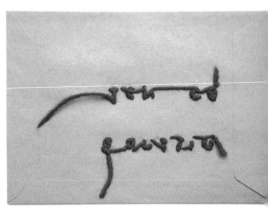

I can't just
stand here
and not say
anything

Jo Taylor

thisisjo.com

United Kingdom

London-based artist Jo Taylor's
handmade postcards are created
by stitching texts onto envelopes
with wool. The backs of the cards
are shown on the right.

Taxi Studio

Art Direction: Alex Bane

and Spencer Buck

Design Direction: Ryan Wills

Design: Roger Whipp

Client: Self-initiated / Integralis

taxistudio.co.uk

United Kingdom

The Taxi Studio Christmas card
for 2006 was created in-house
using two rubber stamps on
recycled cardboard boxes that
had been cut into rectangles.
The purpose of this handmade
creation was both to save trees,
and to donate the money usually
spent on self-promotion during
the holiday season to a much
worthier cause.

Sorry but No Specially Printed
Christmas Card this year. Instead
we thought a sizable donation
to our charity (the NSPCC) would
be a much better idea. Have a
fantastic Christmas and new year,
we look forward to seeing you
in 2007. Love from Alex, Clare,
Hannah, Jo, Karl, Lids, Olly, Phil,
Ryan & Spencer x x x

taxi studio ltd

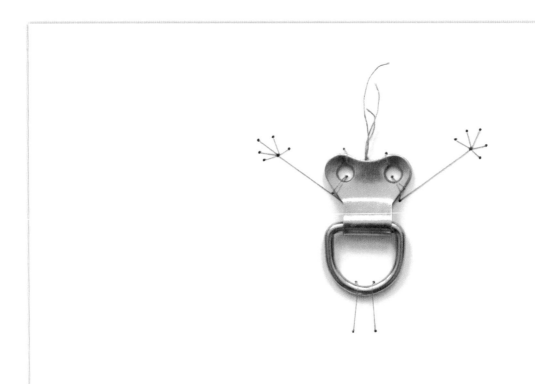

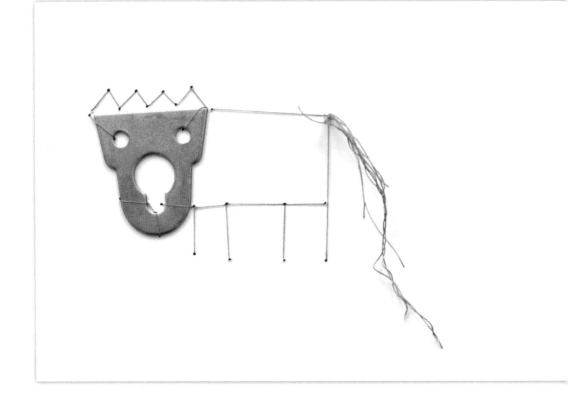

Design: Agathe Jacquillat

and Tomi Vollauschek

flat33.com

United Kingdom

The annual postcard exhibition and fundraising sale at London's Royal College of Art (*RCA Secret*) features original works of art for as little as £40 (US $80). Viewers are invited to guess the artists of the approximately 2,500 cards on display – and must pretend not to be disappointed if they mistake a FL@33 card (such as those featured here) for a Damien Hirst or a David Bowie...

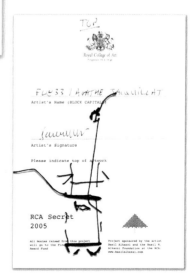

FL@33

Design: Agathe Jacquillat

and Tomi Vollauschek

flat33.com

United Kingdom

A FL@33 white felt contribution
from 2006 to the annual *RCA
Secret* exhibition and fundraising
sale at London's Royal College
of Art.

WISHING YOU PEACE ON EARTH DAY

Celebrate with flowers: Soak this card in water, tear it up, and spread it out on the ground (or in a pot) under a thin layer of soil. Water gently and regularly, keeping the paper moist and out of direct sunlight until the seedlings are well established (1-3 weeks).

S3

Art Direction: Steve Juliano

Copywriter: Denise McVey

s3s3s3.com

USA

behind creating the postcard was to initiate an Earth Day mailing campaign without wasting any paper: upon receiving the postcard, recipients can soak the card in water, tear it up, plant it and finally – watch it grow.

This postcard (left) by agency S3 is printed on a specialty paper that is embedded with seeds. The idea

United States of the Art

Design: Jens Uwe Meyer

and Carsten Raffel

unitedstatesoftheart.com

Germany

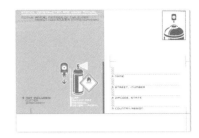

Hamburg-based Carsten Raffel (aka 'Cargo') and Jens Uwe Meyer (aka 'Jum') created virtual studio United States of the Art (USotA). Both founders studied visual communication in Germany, (at Hildesheim and Bielefeld respectively). The stencil card shown here is an example of an innovative reinvention of the postcard – one that defies its simply practical purpose.

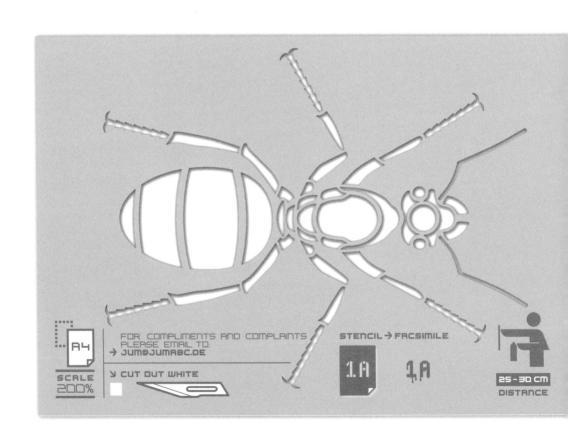

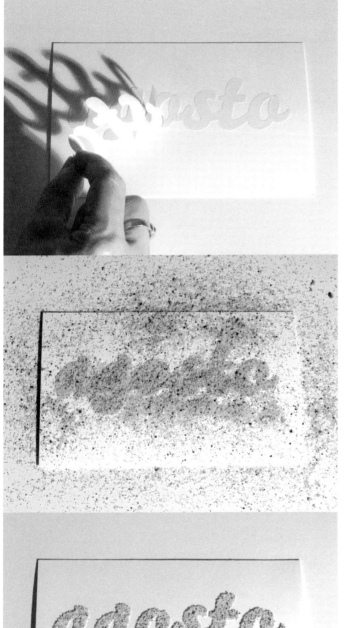

pilargorriz.com

Spain

Barcelona-based studio Pilar Gorriz, Diseño Grafico designed this striking typographic card *Agosto* (August) as a mailshot to communicate to clients that the studio is closed during the month. The card was created using double-sided adhesive tape and real sand.

Detail. Design Studio

Client: Rock N Roll Rescue Squad

detail.ie

Ireland

These 'Vox Pop' flyers are
promotional postcards for a
club night run by client The Rock
N Roll Rescue Squad. One side
features a 'naked' performer,
which recipients are invited to
dress according to their
personal musical tastes using the
stickers provided on the reverse
of the card.

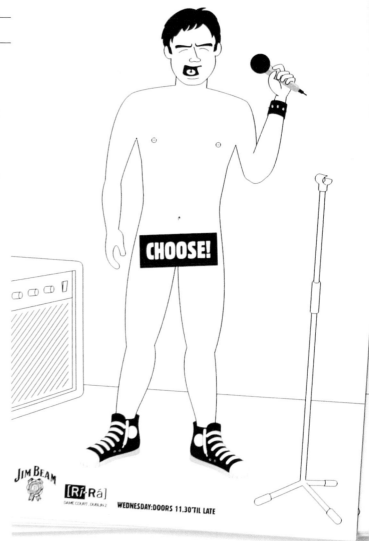

CHOOSE!

JIM BEAM

[Rí-Rá]
GAME COURT, DUBLIN 2   WEDNESDAY:DOORS 11.30'TIL LATE

Perception

Art Direction: Jeremy Lasky

Design: Danielle Palmstrom

perceptionnyc.com

USA

Peel 'n' Stick is a self-promotional postcard for New York City-based Perception. Taking its inspiration from VHS labels, Peel 'n' Stick postcards announce Perception's newly-completed work.

ENTER THE BIZARRE WORLD OF
MECHANICAL PEOPLE & ARTIFICIAL BEASTS
JUNE 22-SEPTEMBER 30, 2005
EXHIBITION & FESTIVAL AT THE ARK
A Cultural Centre for Children, 11a Eustace Street, Temple Bar, Dublin 2
BOOKING: Telephone_ 01 670 7788_ or online at_ www.robots.ie
www.robots.ie

Detail. Design Studio

Client: The Ark

detail.ie

Ireland

These die-cut, pop-up postcards
were created for The Ark, a
cultural centre for children, to
promote *Save The Robots*, an
exhibition for children exploring
the bizarre world of robots and
mechanical beasts.

POSTCARDS

This chapter is a showcase for a wide range of contemporary cards, from individual postcards to small sets and, last but not least, some selected gems from the iconic, inspirational and growing collection that Vaughan Oliver at v23 has created since 1985.

0.67

Emmi

Design: Emmi Salonen

emmi.co.uk

United Kingdom

I Have it All is a comment on the excessive consumerism of the holiday season. The New Year cards lead with 'This year I will', and then provide space for resolutions to be handwritten.

Originally from Finland, Emmi Salonen launched her own studio, Emmi, in 2005. Emmi designed this Christmas and New Year card range while working at Fabrica in 2002. The series sold in Fabrica Features shops in Bologna, Italy and Lisbon, Portugal.

Emily Forgot

Design: Emily Alston

emilyforgot.co.uk

United Kingdom

Emily Forgot is the studio of London-based designer and illustrator Emily Alston. These postcards were produced in 2004 to promote the Emily Forgot website, and were created by over-printing graphic icons onto vintage postcards. Design company Aboud Sodano was one of the companies Alston approached after her postcard campaign. They liked the project so much that they commissioned her to produce a card using the same overprinting technique – this time for a Paul Smith bag show taking place in Japan.

Peskimo

Design: Jodie Davis

and David Partington

peskimo.com

United Kingdom

Jodie and David created this
postcard (right) for a 2007
exhibition curated by Lazy Oaf
entitled Monster Burp. The
postcard-sized print was produced
as a limited-edition Gocco
screenprint on thin balsa wood.

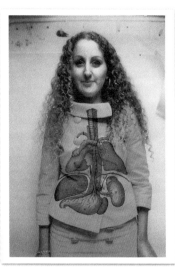

Georgina Potier

georginapotier.com

United Kingdom

London-based illustrator and
designer Georgina Potier receive
a kidney transplant in 1990. Her
work draws heavily on this
experience, and encourages
people to become organ donors
The photographic project shown
here (left) juxtaposes a family
snapshot of Georgina when she
was younger, and a photograph
taken by the photographer Philip
Ebeling in 2004 – which appeared
in the NPG photographic awards
in 2005.

Design: Martin Lorenz

twopoints.net

Spain

Barcelona-based Twopoints.net is run by Martin Lorenz. Shown here are a self-promotional postcard (left), and an invitation to an exhibition (below) for Lorenz' self-initiated project The One Weekend Book series, at the Gallery Ras in Barcelona.

This is a poster announcing a *The One Weekend Book Series* exhibition which will take place at Ras Gallery from the 15th of June until the 15th of July 2007.

FRIDAY, THE 15TH OF JUNE AT 19.00H
Opening Lecture
by Twopoints.Net

FRIDAY, THE 22ND OF JUNE DURING THE WHOLE DAY
TheOneWeekendMovieSeries - Experiment - Part I
directed by Togetheronenomoretime & Twopoints.Net

FRIDAY, THE 29TH OF JUNE DURING THE WHOLE DAY
TheOneWeekendMovieSeries - Experiment - Part II
directed by Togetheronenomoretime & Twopoints.Net

FRIDAY, THE 13TH OF JULY AT 19.00H
TheOneWeekendMovieSeries - Premiere
sound voyage by Lil' jun.

OPENING TIMES / HORARI
Tuesday - Saturday / 11a.m. - 9p.m.
Dimarts - Dissabte / 11:00h - 21:00h

ADDRESS / ADREÇA
Doctor Dou 10
08001 Barcelona

BEST
EDITORIAL
DESIGN

Iceberg

Art Direction and Design:

Simona Castellani

Client: ASUR Marche

iceberg.it

Italy

Aimed at high school students,
these cards, designed by Italian
agency Iceberg for ASUR Marche
(Regional Health Authority),
were part of a campaign to
encourage debate about
social responsibilities. Keywords
featured on the postcards include:
`Life´, `Freedom´, `Happiness´,
`Risk´ and `Responsibility´.

Simon Wild

simonwild.com

United Kingdom

Little Bird is a children's book project by Suffolk-based freelance illustrator Simon Wild. Wild created the project while studying for his MA in Children's Book Illustration at the Cambridge School of Art. Shown here are two installations of the project, whose narrative traces the plight of a little bird looking for a new home. The entire work was exhibited as part of his graduate exhibition in February 2007, and the postcard images now form part of Wild's promotional campaign.

Al Heighton

alanheighton.co.uk

United Kingdom

Self-promotional postcards by artist, designer and illustrator Al Heighton.

Design: James Joyce

one-fine-day.co.uk

United Kingdom

Opposite page: *It's Bigger Than* postcards by London-based artist and designer James Joyce. Pictured here are the postcards that were used to promote a London club night over the span of three years. Each month the illustration on the postcard was animated and projected in the club, creating an evolving showreel of work.

Left: A postcard created for a monthly club night held at The Social, in London. Each month this popular party invites its attendees to *Get Involved* – literally – and distributes instruments to be played throughout the night. An alphabet of letters made from instruments was created to advertise the personality and character of the event.

Below: A set of three postcards commissioned by Carhartt to promote an exhibition showing screenprint installations by James Joyce at their flagship store in Covent Garden, London. The A6-sized cards feature works that were exhibited, and were given away in Carhartt stores.

Julian Morey Studio

Design: Julian Morey

Client: London Cardguide

abc-xyz.co.uk

eklektic.co.uk

United Kingdom

Postcards featuring typographic
designs by London-based
graphic designer and typographer
Julian Morey.

dfuse.com

United Kingdom

These postcards by London-based collective D-Fuse feature some of the highlights of their impressive portfolio, including major collaborative artwork *Undercurrent*, stills from their video installation *Small Global* and onedotzero-produced DVD *D-Tonate_00*.

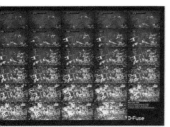

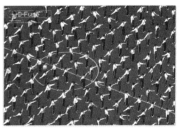

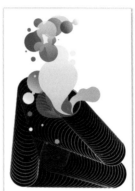

Artiva Design

Design: Daniele de Batté

and Davide Sossi

artiva.it

takeshape.it

danieledebatte.it

Italy

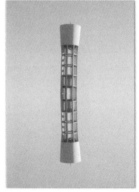

Self-promotion postcards by
Genoa-based studio Artiva Design,
including artwork from the U.F.A.
(Unidentified Flying Architecture)
series. Other works featured here
include *takeshape.it* from a
self-initiated side project, and
Fish, produced for the launch of
Daniele de Batté's website.

Artiva Design

Design: Daniele De Batté

and Davide Sossi

Client: X_Science

artiva.it

Italy

These two *Zoo* postcards were created in 2007 as part of a campaign for X_Science entitled *Cinema tra scienza e fantascienza* (Cinema between science and science fiction), which formed a part of the annual local film festival.

Juju's Delivery

Design: Julia Schonlau

Client: Bizarrverlag

jujus-delivery.com

Germany

Set of four postcards entitled (left, from top down) *Failure, Honest, Pride* and *Simple* featuring characters from the artist's Children of the Revolution series.

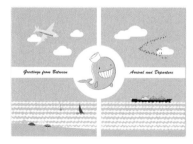

Juju's Delivery

Design: Julia Schonlau

Client: Vanishing Breed

jujus-delivery.com

Germany

Set of five promotional postcards for Vanishing Breed's album release *Between Arrival and Departure* (2005).

...bas

...t Direction and Illustration:

...édric Malo

...ient: Association Orane

...bas.fr

...ance

...arseille-based graphic designer
...bas has been acting as art
...ector of the Marsatac Music
...stival since 2003. The postcards
...own here (right) from 2006 form
...triptych – people are invited to
...llect all three individual
...rds to complete the set. The
...' logo was designed by the
...us des K collective, of which
...bas is a member.

Nils Knoblich

nilsknoblich.com

Germany

The postcard series We Love Kassel
was created exclusively for guests
of the 12th Documenta, Kassel's
acclaimed international annual art
fair. These contemporary picture
postcards of Kassel were designed
by design student Nils Knoblich
and published in collaboration
with rotopolpress.de.

Fluid

Art Direction and Design:

Lee Basford

Client: Adam et Ropé (Japan)

fluidesign.co.uk

United Kingdom

Lee Basford, art director at Birmingham-based agency Fluid designed this set of four limited-edition postcards. Printed on fine art paper, these individually-numbered cards were produced for the 2006 opening of the Meme art project at the Adam et Ropé gallery and clothes store in Shibuya, Tokyo. The four individual cards join to form a single image. All of the shapes and typography are made with hand-cut wood blocks, which were also exhibited during the opening.

A larger print run of two-colour postcards based on the woodcut typography and block shapes of the postcard set was produced for the opening of the Adam et Ropé gallery and clothes store. These were distributed throughout Tokyo in the run-up to the exhibition.

I Make Things

Design: Andrew Groves

imakethings.co.uk

United Kingdom

Promotional postcards by this London-based illustrator and founder of design studio I Make Things. Inspired by the magic of rural Japan, Groves' graphic creations have appeared on postcards, posters, T-shirts, in animation shorts and as mobile phone wallpapers, and his work has been exhibited in London, New York and Tokyo.

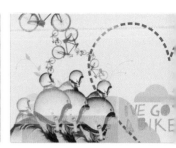

Nazario Graziano

ngdesign.it

Italy

Graziano's colourful and often surreal collages combine photography, hand drawn artwork and striking typography. His work features on websites, posters, postcards and in graphics magazines worldwide, and is available to buy as prints.

Above: Self-initiated artworks by Nazario Graziano.

Right: A selection of postcards Nazario created for Italian night-club Firewater.

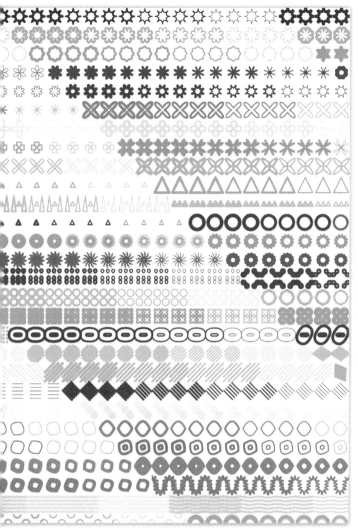

Kapitza

Design: Petra and Nicole Kapitza

kapitza.com

kapitza.com/shop

United Kingdom

London-based sisters Petra and Nicole Kapitza created these postcards to promote two of their studio's self-initiated projects: Portrait Illustration Set Z – a set of 18 individual portrait illustrations of boys and girls in editable vector format – and Pop, one of their decorative fonts.

Pop contains 320 graphic elements in 4 weights (Pop10, Pop20, Pop30, Pop40). When repeated, each Pop element creates a unique pattern which can then be combined into a variety of new patterns. Additionally, each Pop element of one weight can both overlay and combine with its counterparts to generate new variations and patterns.

Hush

studio-hush.com

United Kingdom

These postcards by urban artist Hush are entitled *I luv my vinyl* and were produced in 2007 in a 50-card limited edition. The three-colour, hand-pulled screenprints are signed and numbered by the artist. The A6 postcards – miniature versions of 20 x 28-in (500 x 700-mm) prints produced in the same edition – were mailed to prospective collectors and galleries, as well as being posted in public spaces to attract potential buyers to the recent artworks being exhibited.

nickcannons.co.uk

United Kingdom

This is a self-directed project based on a poem by Bob Auld, a poet from Stevenston, a small town on Scotland's west coast on the Firth of Clyde. London-based graphic designer Nick Cannons designed the postcards as a reaction to the poem's message about small-town British culture: '"*The Cosy Cluster*" *is about a local pub and the characters who frequent it.*'

Daniel Eatock

eatock.com

United Kingdom

Right: Designed in 1998 by London-based graphic designer Dan Eatock while he was studying at the Royal College of Art, this postcard was published in an edition of 1,000 copies. The rubber stamp effect on the card creates the impression of a first-class postage stamp. Each card is stamped by hand.

Left and below: This card (front and back shown) arrived without any postage having been paid.

NO Dropping Litter
NO Urban 4x4's
NO Blocking Cycle Lanes
NO Religion
NO Junk Email
NO Telemarketing
NO Smoking
NO Ignoring People
NO Perfume
NO Dumb Advertising
NO Drink Driving
NO Copying Ideas
NO Objectification
NO Dumping Car Batteries
NO Free Pitches
NO Sugar in Coffee
NO Hitting

NO **STAMP**

T●ml
FL @33
59 BRITTON ST
LONDON
EC1M 5UU

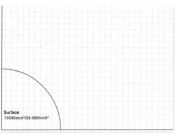

Surface
15540mm²/24.089inch²

Circumference
506mm/19.921inch

Visualdata

Design: Ronald Wisse

visualdata.org

The Netherlands

Amsterdam-based web designer Ronald Wisse continued his 'Anatomy Series' for this book – a series he began in 2006 for a set of 1-in (25-mm) button badges he designed for Stereohype.com.

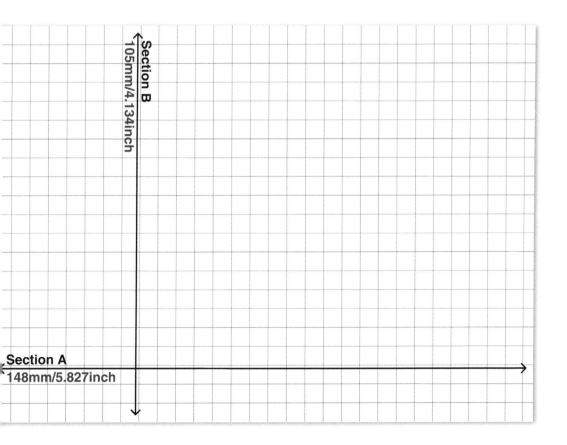

Section B
105mm/4.134inch

Section A
148mm/5.827inch

NogoodCorp

Design: Jordan Nogood

nogoodcorp.com

USA

This humour card was created by California-based artist Jordan Nogood in 2004. The back of the postcard picks up the theme of work that the front artwork introduces, and features basic details about average working hours in America: *'Many people work. Some for fun. Some because they need money. Most people prefer to not be at work. Some people work so much they lose their identity outside of work.'*

Stephen Woowat

woowat.com

Client: Boomerang Media

United Kingdom

Emotional Waste Disposal, a self-proclaimed 'Positive Thinking Campaign', was born from artist Stephen Woowat's final year university project. The postcard was subsequently distributed by Boomerang Media, UK, in 2006.

The back of the card states that *'... we believe that a physical action can reflect your mental state. We encourage you to vent your pessimism and mental demons in a written form, to help purge your mind. So pen down whatever's troubling you, throw away and forget about it.'*

THIS **CARD** HAS BEEN APPROVED FOR
ALL AUDIENCES
BY THE POSTCARD ASSOCIATION OF THE NETHERLANDS, INC.

THE CARD PRINTED HAS BEEN RATED

B	**BORING**	®
	POSTAGE CAN BE PAID USING ANY METHOD EXCEPT PRECANCELED STAMPS	
NO STRONG GRAPHIC VIOLENCE, DISTURBING CONTENT SEXUALITY, NUDITY, DRUG USE OR LANGUAGE		

ᵀM_INC

sign: Danny Geerlof

design.nl/dtm/illus.html

omerang.nl/DTM_INC

ent: Boomerang Media

e Netherlands

ring by Danny Geerlof is from a
nge of postcards created over a
riod of time for Boomerang
edia, and parodies the classic
tem of rating movies.

Graphic Oil

Design: Lasko

graphicoil.com

Client: Boomerang Media

The Netherlands

This card was produced for
Boomerang in the Netherlands.
Designed by Lasko at Graphic Oil,
the artwork commemorates the
killing of well-known Dutch writer
and film director Theo van Gogh
in Amsterdam.

Airside

Design: Jamie Wieck

airside.co.uk

United Kingdom

Jamie Wieck from London-based design studio Airside comments on his postcard caricature of the queen (above): 'Our good Queen has many uses: addressing the nation, opening parliament and keeping an eye on Prince Philip – but on a postcard, quite frankly we think she's wasted. Our postcard design puts the Queen's noble portrait to good use, and in a way that is tantamount to treason – who said we never suffered for our art... '

Rod Hunt

rodhunt.com

United Kingdom

Inspired by retro graphics and contemporary culture, Hunt's vibrant digital illustrations focus on people and cityscapes. This self-promotional postcard is entitled 'B-Movie City' and features 21 movie references within it. Hunt has been commissioned to create work for a vast array of companies ranging from corporate clients to newspapers and TV companies.

Zeptonn

Design: Stinger aka

Jan Willem Wennekes

zeptonn.nl

The Netherlands

Self-promotional postcards
by Groningen-based Zeptonn.
Former student of philosophy, the
designer tries to convey joy and
happiness in his work and is
inspired by monsters, street art,
colour and wacky situations.

Christian Ward

christianward.co.uk

United Kingdom

London-based illustrator Christian Ward achieves his unique stylistic effect by first colouring his hand-drawn artwork with pro-markers, and then finishing them in Photoshop. *Pomme Pomme Rabbit* (above) was produced especially for this book, while *Clockwork A* (left) is a self-promotional card.

AN ABOVE THE TITLE PRODUCTION

Chloe

"BEING RICH AND FAMOUS
AND MUCH-LOVED, AND NOT
GIVING A FIG. IT'S THE MANNER
IN WHICH I'VE ACHIEVED IT
THAT MATTERS TO ME..."

AN ABOVE THE TITLE PRODUCTION

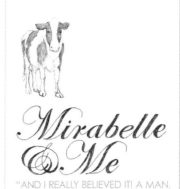

Mirabelle & Me

"AND I REALLY BELIEVED IT! A MAN,
AND A BULLOCK, IN A GARAGE IN
SUBURBIA. NO PROBLEM, SURELY?"

AN ABOVE THE TITLE PRODUCTION

on the blog

'YOU'VE HEARD OF
RADIO ON THE INTERNET...
NOW GET READY FOR
THE INTERNET ON RADIO"

AN ABOVE THE TITLE PRODUCTION

THE HARDER THEY FALL

"YOU KNOW THE FIGHT BUSINESS.
IT'S SHOW BUSINESS WITH BLOOD."
BUDD SCHULBERG

AN ABOVE THE TITLE PRODUCTION

CHICKEN No.23 INSPECTOR
THE STORY OF S.J. PERELMAN

"FROM THE MOMENT I PICKED UP
YOUR BOOK UNTIL I LAID IT DOWN,
WAS CONVULSED WITH LAUGHTER.
SOMEDAY I INTEND READING IT."
GROUCHO MARX

AN ABOVE THE TITLE PRODUCTION

CLIVE ANDERSON'S CHATROOM

"FAT IS CHEWED, IDEAS ARE
KICKED AROUND, THE TOSS IS
ARGUED" CLIVE ANDERSON

Marc&Anna

Design: Marc Atkinson,

Anna Ekelund and Connie Wright

Client: Above The Title

marcandanna.co.uk

United Kingdom

This selection from a series of
postcards by London-based
graphic design consultancy
Marc&Anna was initially produced
for radio production company
Above The Title to promote their
forthcoming productions. Each
card's stylistic features include a
pencil drawing, hand-rendered
type, a quotation from the
programme and a brief synopsis
of the plot.

Sub Communications

Design: Valérie Desrochers

subcommunication.com

subtitude.com

Canada

This Christmas card from Montréal-based creative production and consultancy company Sub Communications, features their dingbat font Suboel by Subtitude Foundry.

Marcela Alejandra

marcelaalejandra.com

United Kingdom

A self-promotional card by Marcelo Alejandra, a recent graduate from the Royal College of Art, which was featured in a group exhibition promoting the work of emerging artists. Alejandra works in a range of media, from ballpoints, fiber tips and crayons to acrylics and collage, and favours fluorescent and iridescent inks.

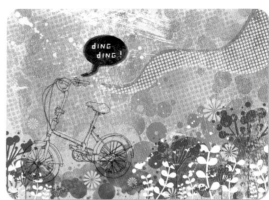

lderness

esign: Kat Stubbings

derness.com

tstubbings.com

ited Kingdom

s artwork cleverly uses the first
o letters of the word 'optimism'
form the eyes and nose of a
iling face, and was created
London-based Illustrator Kat
bbings for her company
derness. Her distinctive style of
stration mixes detailed linework
h splashes of colour and bold
ography, and her work has
tured on packaging, T-shirts,
nts and in animation shorts.

Yee Ting Kuit

yeellustration.co.uk

United Kingdom

Freelance illustrator Yee Ting Kuit
produced this postcard as part
of a pack of promotional items
that were sent out to potential
clients. Featured on the card is
an illustration based on the theme
of alternative transport that Kuit
created in response to an open
brief for *Amelia's Magazine*.

Gastón Liberto

gastonliberto.blogspot.com

myspace.com/libertoarte

Spain

This delicate watercolour series by Barcelona-based Gastón Liberto is called Melancholy of Modernity. Born in Argentina, his work is influenced by Latin American culture, magic and surrealism, and he is inspired by the circus and carnivals.

Could you be as kind as to save my life ?

Javier González Burgos

illustrationartworks.blogspot.com

javiergbilustraciones.blogspot.com

Argentina

These two cards by Buenos Aires-based illustrator Javier González Burgos are from his series Finding Things – Don't Know What To Do.

www.inksurge.com

Inksurge

Design: Rex Advincula

and Joyce Tai

Client: People Like Us Collective

inksurge.com

Philippines

Left: People Like Us Collective invited Inksurge to design a shirt for their new white T-shirt line. Postcards such as the one featured here accompany each T-shirt purchase.

Katharina Leuzinger

Client: Rainbow Trust

katleuzinger.com

United Kingdom

Below: Postcards for the Rainbow Trust Children's Charity, in collaboration with Studio Thomson and Major Players.

katleuzinger.com

United Kingdom

Self-promotional cards by London-based artist Katharina Leuzinger. Raised in Switzerland by Swiss and Japanese parents, Leuzinger is influenced by both cultures and is known for her playful and colourful work, crisp graphics and decisive use of colour.

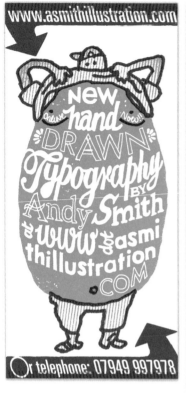

Andy Smith

asmithillustration.com

United Kingdom

Above: This silkscreen-printed postcard by London-based Illustrator Andy Smith promotes his self-published book *Fatty's Big Bubble*.

All other cards are printed on litho and are used to promote Andy's artwork.

Sofia Morais

sofiamorais.net

Portugal

In 2003 Lisbon-based graphic designer Sofia Morais took part in the European Union's youth programme European Voluntary Service (EVS). Along with other European volunteers, Sophia lived and worked in Spoleto, Italy, where they produced a magazine for the young inhabitants of Spoleto. The postcards shown here document the intensity, positivity and multi-culturalism that characterized the project. The cards were sponsored by the European Community in 2006 and distributed across Europe.

Elfen

Design: Aaron Easterbrook

and Guto Evans

Photography: Huw Talfryn Walters

Client: Volcano Theatre Company

elfen.co.uk

United Kingdom

Cardiff-based design studio Elfen
created these cards as part of
promotional material for the show
A Few Little Drops, about the all
consuming properties of water. The
designers aimed to reflect the
philosophy of the show by shooting
various objects under water.

Lucas Ballocchi

brocoli.cl

Chile

These postcards by graphic designer Lucas Ballocchini were created after a Chilean friend asked him to clarify the difference between the English word 'sale' and Spanish word *salé* – which means 'leave'. The cards are also a response to the constant presence and use of American colloquialisms and words in Chilean advertising.

Mr Bowlegs

Design: Jeffrey Bowman

mrbowlegs.co.uk

United Kingdom

Left: Front and back of a postcard by design graduate Jeffrey Bowman. The artwork is defined by an anti-gravity theme.

Yoki

yoki-lab.com

France

My Brand Project

peter-wendy.com

France

Rosanna Traina

rosietraina.blogspot.com

rosanna.traina@alumni.rca.ac.uk

United Kingdom

Paris-based graphic designer
Yoki created this artwork for an
exhibition which took place in
June 2007 at the Artcore Gallery,
in Paris.

This is one of many postcards
created for the travelling exhibition
My Brand Project. Initiated in
2004 and curated by Paris-based
Xavier Encinas (formerly known
as Rumbero Design) and Cécilia
Michaud, the highly successful
exhibition also features a variety
of merchandise.

Produced to accompany the
Communication Art and Design
MA graduation show at the Royal
College of Art in 2007, this self-
promotional card features
characters from Carnival and
All-Right!, two of Rosanna Traina'
original typefaces.

lex Robbins

exrobbins.co.uk

ited Kingdom

Jamie Wood

dubpixel.co.uk

United Kingdom

Kate Sutton

katesutton.co.uk

United Kingdom

oduced after a hectic day
·h his colouring pencils, Alex
bbins sent out this postcard
promote his 2007 work.

London-based graphic designer
and illustrator Jamie Wood
created the *Crash Rhino* to
promote a club night in Den Haag,
the Netherlands. The project was
initiated by the club's DJ and
the result has seen a surge of
interest in the club night.

A self-promotional postcard by
illustrator Kate Sutton. Inspired by
children's books and nature, her
cute and kitsch illustrations have
appeared on T-shirts, websites,
prints and textiles.

Virtual Typography

Design: Matthias Hillner

virtualtypography.com

United Kingdom

Created in 2006 by London-based graphic designer Matthias Hillner and his studio Virtual Typography, this postcard features Hillner's own Gravita font.

Monica Fraile

monica.fraile.free.fr

France

Postcard by Paris-based graphic designer Monica Fraile. Her simple and striking, largely typographic designs use a limited palette and have appeared on numerous posters, logos, books and CDs.

Marcus Diamond

marcusdiamond.com

United Kingdom

Self-promotional postcard from freelance artist Marcus Diamond who also co-founded the Neasd Control Centre.

olourbox

esign: Joe Rogers

olourboxshop.bigcartel.com

nited Kingdom

onig von Nichts (King of Nothing) as initially produced in response an article about money ublished in the Spanish cultural agazine *Lamono*. The card was eated by Birmingham-based Joe ogers and his studio Colourbox.

BC, MH

Design: Ben Chatfield

and Mark Hopkins

Photography: Clare Shilland

bcmh.co.uk

United Kingdom

This self-promotional postcard *Boo* is the work of Ben Chatfield and Mark Hopkins, the two founders of London-based graphic design studio BC, MH.

Agnese Bicocchi

agnesbic.com

United Kingdom

London-based illustrator Agnese Bicocchi drew inspiration for the postcard above from the Croatian town of Zadar. She dedicated the work to the town: '*Down there, people dive from marble steps, swim next to city walls and someone even built a sea organ...*'

www.musacollective.com Original design for Laundry, Japan.
http://www.laundry038.com

**Say Hello: MusaCollectiveTour
Tokyo/JAPAN—2006**
Sponsored by Laundry

Musa:
Portuguese
DesignCollective™

Say Hello: MusaCollectiveTour
Tokyo/JAPAN—2006

Musa

Design: Raquel Viana, Paulo Lima

and Ricardo Alexandre

musacollective.com

Portugal

Promotional postcards for the acclaimed MusaCollective Tours – a travelling annual exhibition by Portugese design collective Musa to showcase the work of Portugese graphic designers and help to give the country a design identity.

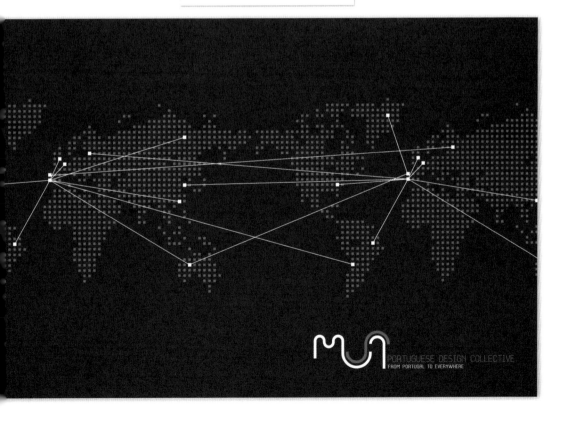

FL@33

Design: Agathe Jacquillat

Client: Jean-Charles de

Castelbajac

flat33.com

United Kingdom

Pre-FL@33 postcards *Escape* and
Life is beautiful were created for
Jean-Charles de Castelbajac's
concept store in Paris in 1999.

Design: Agathe Jacquillat

and Tomi Vollauschek

flat33.com

United Kingdom

Showcased here are some of the promotional cards created for FL@33's sister-company Stereohype.com.

Opposite page, top: *Stereohype Button Badge Collection*. Created between October 2004 and June 2006, the badges feature artwork by designers and artists from around the world.

Left and Below: Stereohype *Squirrel* cards from 2006 and 2004 respectively.

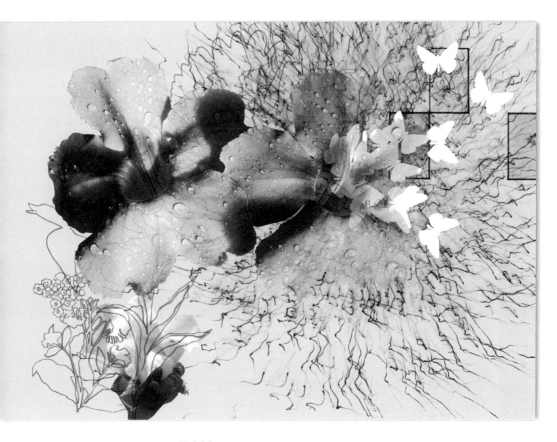

FL@33

Design: Agathe Jacquillat

and Tomi Vollauschek

flat33.com

United Kingdom

Above: FL@33 Postcard *#4 Spring*, published in 2003. This is a detail from an A1-sized poster featured in the FL@33 monograph. This mixed-media artwork combines photographic elements, vector artwork and details from hand-drawn sketches.

Opposite page:
Top: FL@33 postcard *#5 Shadows, passers-by seen from Eiffel Tower*, published in 2006.
This illustration features numerous cut-out photographs taken from passers-by seen from the Eiffel Tower. People and their shadows were not modified but were simply turned to feature vertical shadows and thus create a surreal perspective.

Bottom: FL@33 postcard *#2 Envelope Pattern*, published in 2002. This design was created for use as FL@33 stationery.

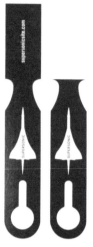

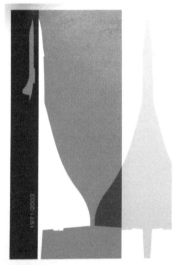

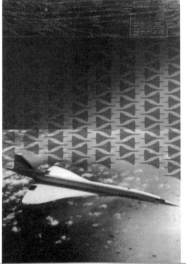

LAD

Design: Lawrence Azerrad

laddesign.net

supersonicsite.com

USA

This tri-fold postcard features three artworks designed by Los Angeles-based Lawrence Azerrad Design. The artworks were designed specifically for the Supersonic event, an exhibition exploring the history, technology, lifestyle and design of the Concorde. Copies of this postcard and a black satin Supersonic sleep mask were presented to each of the guests on the exhibition's opening night.

Stoltze Design

Design: Clifford Stoltze

and Roy Burns

Client: AIGA

stoltze.com

USA

Boston-based Stoltze Design
created the 2005 AIGA
Fellows Award invitation
along with these four postcards,
which accompanied the
design industry invitation.

as loud as hell
a ringing bell
behind my smile
it shakes my teeth

v23

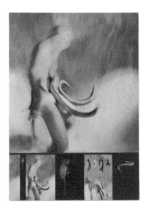

Client: 4AD

v-23.co.uk

United Kingdom

The following six pages feature a few rare postcards with visuals by the inspirational London-based graphic designer Vaughan Oliver and his v23 collaborators. Selected cards were published between 1985 and 2005.

Opposite page, top: Picture from the cover booklet of the Pixies' *Doolittle* album (1989), and detail from the record sleeve of Pixies' *Gigantic/River Euphrates* (1988). Photography: Simon Larbalestier

Opposite page, bottom: Postcard from The Breeders' *Pod* album (1990). Photography: Kevin Westenberg

Left: Created by Vaughan Oliver (23 envelope), for the Pixies' *Surfer Rosa* album (1988). Photography: Simon Larbalestier

Below: Promotional postcards for the release of the Pixies' single 'Debaser'.

Design : Vaughan Oliver at v23
Photography : Steph / Kjal & Anderson

gusgus

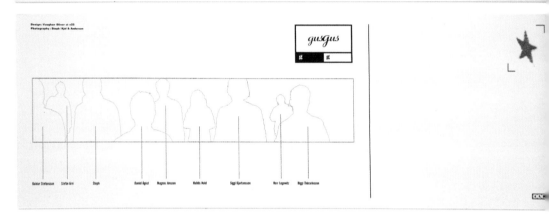

Bakfar Stefansson   Stefan Arni   Steph   Daniel Agacil   Magnus Jonsson   Maldis Hold   Siggi Kjartansson   Herr Legowitz   Biggi Thoracleosson

DOC

Client: 4AD

v-23.co.uk

United Kingdom

Left: Detail from the record sleeve from *Ultra Vivid Scene* (1988) and 4AD invitation to a preview screening of video *Toward the Within* by Dead Can Dance (1994). Art Direction: Chris Bigg, Photography: Linda Connor

Below: Cards announcing the release of albums *The Comfort Of Madness* by Pale Saints (1990) and *Polydistortion* by GusGus (1997). Art Direction and Design: Vaughan Oliver and Chris Bigg Photography: Paul Bliss

Opposite page, top: Oversized panoramic postcard (30 cm (12 in) wide) introducing the band members of GusGus. Photography: Steph, Kjól Anderson

Opposite page, bottom: Seasonal postcards for the following single releases by Lush: '500 (Shake by Shake)', 'Single Girl' and 'Ladykillers' (1996). Photography: Ichiro Kono

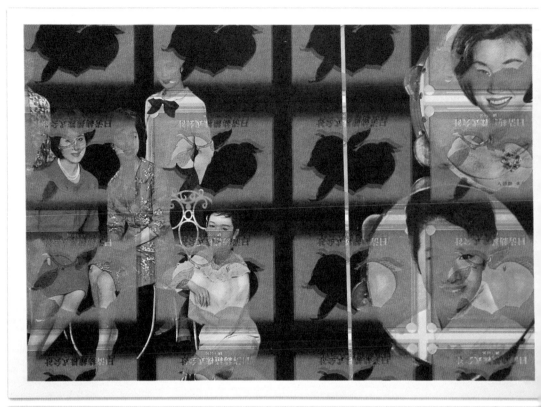

v23

v-23.co.uk

United Kingdom

Opposite page, top: Number 7 in a series of 12 cards designed by 23 envelope for the Colourbox album released by record label 4AD (1985).

Opposite page, bottom: Detail from the *Design in post-war Japan* poster for the V&A Museum in London.
Design: Vaughan Oliver and Chris Bigg at v23

Top, left: Artwork from Fields of the Nephilim's 'For Her Light' single release from the *Elyzium* album (1990) produced by Beggars Banquet Records.
Design: Chris Bigg at v23,
Photography: Beverley Carruthers

Top, right: *Glove* artwork for the Vaughan Oliver and v23 exhibition at the DDD Gallery in Osaka, Japan, in 1992.
Photography: Dominic Davies

Left and below: Five postcards produced in 2005 for independent record label 4AD's 25th anniversary shows.

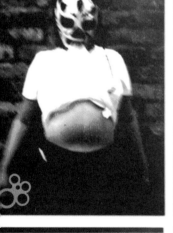

BOOKS AND SETS

This section features extraordinarily well-designed examples of collaborative art. Many of these projects began as joint efforts by design collectives and individuals, and became bound, limited-edition books, concertina folds and sets featuring anything from four to one million pieces.

1.25

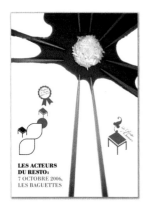

LES ACTEURS DU RESTO:
7 OCTOBRE 2006,
LES BAGUETTES

LES ACTEURS
DU RESTO:
4 FÉVRIER 2006
LA VAISSELLE
DE DESSERT

LES ACTEURS
DU RESTO:
4 MARS 2006,
LES COUVERTS

LES ACTEURS
DU RESTO:
5 MAI 2006,
LES VERRES

LES ACTEURS
DU RESTO:
4 NOVEMBRE 2006,
LES ASSIETTES

10 JUIN 2006,
LES BOLS

ANVIER 2007:
NKE

Monokini

Design: Nathalie Imhof

and Marlène Jeannerat

Client: Resto d'Occases

monokini.ch

Switzerland

Promotional postcards by
Lausanne-based Monokini
for restaurant Resto d'Occases.

2 JUIN 2007:
LISE

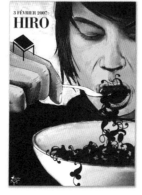

3 FÉVRIER 2007:
HIRO

3 MARS 2007:
MONA

21 AVRIL 2007:
LENA

Hat-trick

Creative Direction: Gareth Howat, David Kimpton and Jim Sutherland

Design: Ben Christie

Client: Land Securities

hat-trickdesign.co.uk

United Kingdom

FTSE 100 company Land Securities are London's leading property developers. The focus of their Capital Knowledge campaign highlights a unique knowledge of London: Hat-trick design was commissioned to produce a range of postcards (of which a selection is shown here), each displaying an archaic law still in force in London. The postcards were used to promote the new campaign internally.

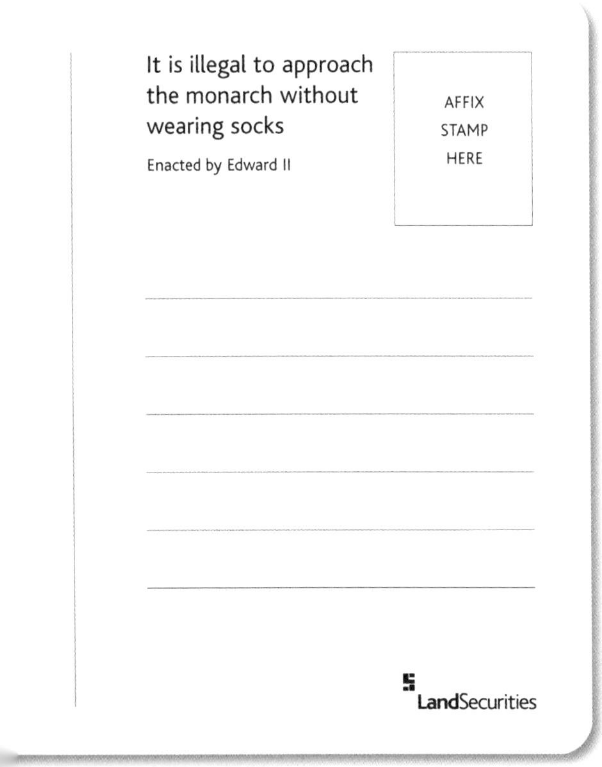

It is illegal to approach the monarch without wearing socks

Enacted by Edward II

AFFIX
STAMP
HERE

LandSecurities

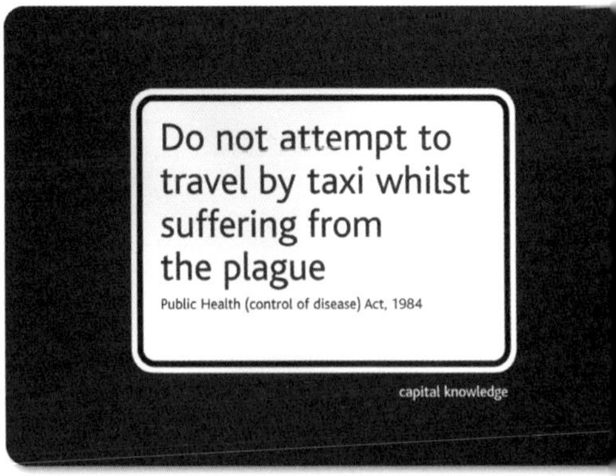

Do not attempt to travel by taxi whilst suffering from the plague

Public Health (control of disease) Act, 1984

capital knowledge

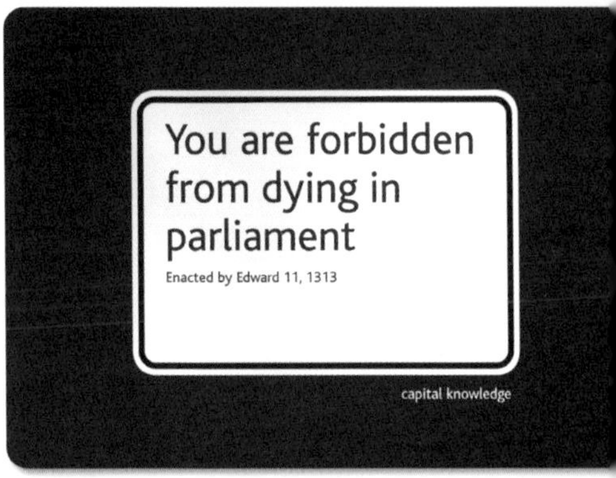

You are forbidden from dying in parliament

Enacted by Edward 11, 1313

capital knowledge

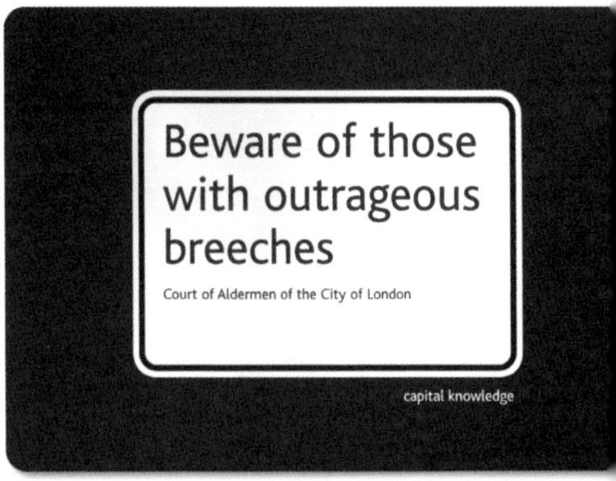

Beware of those with outrageous breeches

Court of Aldermen of the City of London

capital knowledge

You may face imprisonment if discovered drunk in charge of a steam engine or a cow.

The Licensing Act, 1972

capital knowledge

Mark Adams

markadamsimages.com

United Kingdom

Manchester-based Mark Adams is a photographic artist who graduated from London's Royal College of Art in 2001. This perforated series (above), entitled Postcards from America, was available during the final year RCA exhibition.

Top row, left to right: *Gas Station*: New Orleans, Louisiana; *Flower Bed*: Las Vegas, Nevada; *Cemetery*: Galveston, Texas
Middle row, left to right: *Suburban House*: Halfmoon Bay, California; *Parking Lot*: New Orleans, Louisiana; *Elections*: Galveston, Texas
Bottom row, left to right: *Billboard*: Interstate 10, Texas; *Manhattan*: Las Vegas, Nevada; *$39*: Interstate 15, Nevada

Adam Brickles

superskint.co.uk

United Kingdom

Adam Brickles obtained an MA in Communication Design from London's Central Saint Martins in 2007. His work combines materials gathered over a two-year period with text. Themes include the similarities between football and religion, both the obsessive nature of worshippers and their use of song.

Craig Salter at Wolseley

Art Direction: Craig Salter

Design: Craig Salter, Dan Eagling
and Ed Evans

Client: Build Centre (Wolseley UK)

salter.cd@btopenworld.com

United Kingdom

In 2004 Build Centre (which is
part of the Wolseley UK group)
sponsored the Masters Football
event, an event which saw ex
top-flight football players return to
the field in a 5-a-side tournament.
Craig Salter and the rest of the
Wolseley in-house design team
created postcards to promote
the event. In total 24 postcards
were created – one per team –
each featuring an iconic player
of the last 20 years.

25 December   **1** January   **20** February   **17** March

14 April   **7** May   **17** June   **16** July

27 August   **8** September   **31** October   **11** November

A2 Design

Art Direction: Andrew Pengilly

Design & Research: Daniel Cullinan

a2design.co.uk

United Kingdom

A2 created this set of postcards as a self-promotional mailer, which was sent out monthly throughout 2007. The concept behind the aptly-named Traditions series is to reveal the origins behind different British traditions. Illustrated as visual puzzles, traditions depicted include *Star of Bethlehem, New Year's Day, Pancake Day, Saint Patrick's Day, First Cuckoo Day, May Day, Father's Day, Swan Upping, Bank*

Holiday, Last Night of The Proms, Halloween, Remembrance Day.

Airside

airside.co.uk

United Kingdom

London-based design company Airside created these postcards for an exhibition of their work held in Tokyo, in 2005. The postcards were distributed as mementos of the Airside exhibit, which included two customized interactive installations, animations and prints. The postcards showcase various aspects of Airside's work, including character design (Dot Coms), product design (Stitches) and illustration.

Toy2R

toy2r.com

Hong Kong

Art company Toy2R draws artists from all over the world, creating the global artist network that gave birth to worldwide phenomenon Qee toys, one of the world's hottest pop culture collectibles. The BuneeQ alone has attracted multiple new artists and customizers to the toy industry. One hundred and six customized vinyl toys were selected for publication in two limited-edition postcard books following a worldwide toy exhibition. *Toy2R Bunny Qee Fiesta 1* and *2* respectively feature 50 and 56 postcards which can be torn out and sent.

Concrete Hermit

Design: Andrew James Jones

concretehermit.com

United Kingdom

Leaks by Andrew James Jones was the second in a growing series of postcard books published by London-based Chris Knight and his company Concrete Hermit. 'A right twisted little book', read one review. After *Leaks* sold out completely, Concrete Hermit and Andrew began compiling a second collection of work.

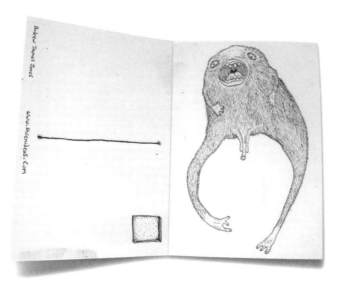

Concrete Hermit

Design: Jon Burgerman

concretehermit.com

United Kingdom

Concrete Hermit

Design: Hellovon

concretehermit.com

United Kingdom

Postcard book *Sweaty Goolabs* (2007) contains a range of artist Jon Burgerman's work, from doodles on post-it notes and envelopes to photos and more elaborately rendered pieces. The book was published by Concrete Hermit, whose founder Chris Knight is a long-term collaborator of Burgerman's: *'Jon Burgerman is well known for his unique and colourful artwork – both commercial and personal projects have seen Jon's "doodles" on scraps of paper, cardboard, canvas, walls and objects.'*

The postcard book *Von* by Hellovon was published in 2007 by Concrete Hermit. Founder Chris Knight comments on Von's particular stylistic blend of traditional and digital mark-making techniques: *'His style is quite different from some of the artists we'd worked with before. I'd seen an exhibition of his and in particular it was an illustration of the pop duo Daphne and Celeste (who had a hit with "Oh Stick You!"), which made me want to work with him.'*

oncrete Hermit

esign: Ian Stevenson

oncretehermit.com

nited Kingdom

ut Up Man by Ian Stevenson
as the very first in the series of
ostcard books published by
oncrete Hermit. Released in 2005
e edition was jointly funded by
e artist, and sold out completely.
oncrete Hermit founder Chris
ight explains of Shut Up Man:
*he character "The Shut Up Man"
sponds to 22 different
atements. These were things
eople would say to which
u'd quite rightly think "Shut Up!"'*

Concrete Hermit

Design: Ian Stevenson

concretehermit.com

United Kingdom

Lost Heroes (2006), the second
postcard book by Ian Stevenson
sold out entirely. The narrative
connecting each of the depicted
characters in the book was born
from an idea that Stevenson had
about actors auditioning for
cartoon character roles – and
failing. *'Lost Heroes catches up
with them to see what they've
been up to since failing
to find stardom. Seeing Ian's
twisted characters is enough
to understand why they were
never given the staring roles!'*,
explains Concrete Hermit founder,
Chris Knight.

Concrete Hermit

Design: Motomichi

concretehermit.com

United Kingdom

Monstruos & Maestros by
Motomichi was released in 2007.
Chris Knight, whose company
Concrete Hermit published the
book, first encountered Motomichi

at the Pictoplasma conference in
Berlin. Their meeting spurred a
collaboration on T-shirt design,
as well as on the red, black and
white monsters pictured above.
Knight comments that *'it's the
inclusion of one photographic
image in the middle of this book
that makes it work.'*

oncrete Hermit

esign: Skwak

oncretehermit.com

nited Kingdom

e self-titled postcard book
Skwak was published in 2006.
oncrete Hermit expressed
terest in publishing a collection
the artist's work after seeing
e colourful characters splattered
cross Skwak's website.

Concrete Hermit

Design: Andrew Rae

concretehermit.com

United Kingdom

Andrew Rae's ability `to somehow
(he can) make a man with a
dog's head spearing a strange
little creature seem like a perfectly
normal, everyday occurrence'
first attracted Chris Knight, founder
of Concrete Hermit, to compile
and publish a selection of his
postcards. Of Beasts And
Machines was released in 2006.

1503
autumn-winter
collection

1826
spring-summer
collection

1942
autumn-winter
collection

1970
spring-summer
collection

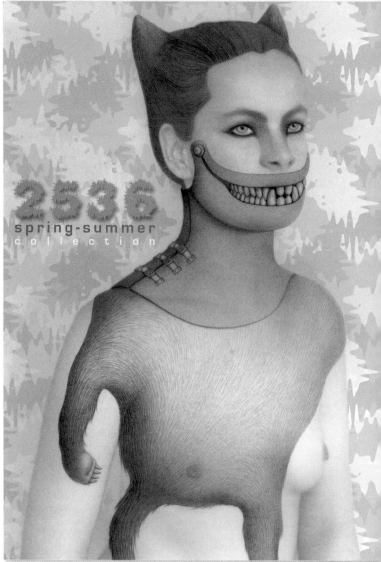

2536
spring-summer
collection

Model: Diane

garance.margot@free.fr

France

Paris-based Garance Margot created these images in 2002 to exhibit at the Estivales Photographiques du Trégor in Lannion, France. Working with the exhibition theme of 'A fleu de peau' ('sensitive to the skin') Garance created 30 black and white photos from drawings on tracing paper. Each artwork explores the idea that 'l'habit fait le moine', or 'clothes make the man', from a different point in history. Garance colourized six of the cards especially for this book.

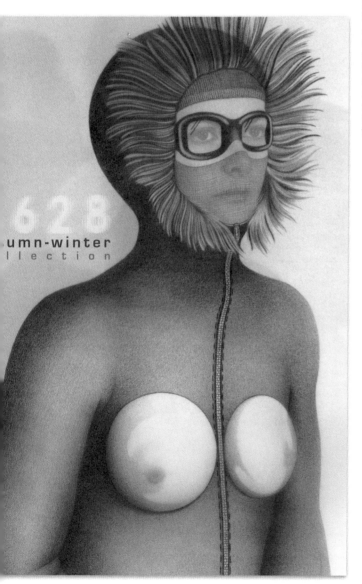

catalinaestrada.com

Spain

Catalina Estrada was born and raised in Colombia and has been living in Barcelona since 1999. Invoking the powerful colour of Latin-American folklore in her art, she refines all of her work to a sophisticated finish. Presented here are two of her postcard series, Boys and Girls, featuring a collection of characters created between 2005 and 2006, and El Jardin (The Garden), which was created for a solo exhibition in Colombia in 2005.

Holger Lübbe

holgerluebbe.de

Germany

This postcard series marked the beginning of Holger Lübbe's ongoing Give and Take project. Equipped with a large-format Linhof Technika camera and Polaroid Typ 55 material, Holger travelled to Lulekani, a Township in the northeast of South Africa, to work with the Leka Gape charity. The photo material – consisting mostly of portraits of locals and snapshots of their everyday life – creates an instant positive black and white Polaroid print as well as a negative. This dual process allows Lübbe to give away Polaroid prints to amazed locals, while retaining negatives – which are later developed into the material the charity uses to help source potential European sponsors. The project has since been adopted in other parts of the world.

footprintsinthesnow.co.uk

United Kingdom

This postcard set by Manchester-based Rick Myers features excerpts from the 1997–2003 *Footprints in the Snow* catalogue. This is an ongoing catalogue of his graphic work, which has included designing record sleeves, posters and art prints as well as directing videos.

Koa Dzn

Design: Olivier Cramm, aka

Koa and Romuald at The Lazy Dog

koadzn.com

thelazydog.fr

France

Koa is a Lille-based designer and illustrator. He initiated *War of Monstars* – a postcard book featuring 80 colourful cards – and joined forces with The Lazy Dog to edit the publication. The book showcases the 80 graphic designers and illustrators from around the world that Koa invited to fight him in a graphic battle based on the theme of monster films, or `kaiju`. The resulting collaborative artworks feature Koa's monsters fighting the creatures of his selected participants. Postcards featured here are Koa versus: *Himself, Strom, Flying Fortress, Evaq, Huskmitnavn, Hydro 74, Sunny, Madbarbarians, Marc Digart, Rinzen, Skull* and *Veenom*.

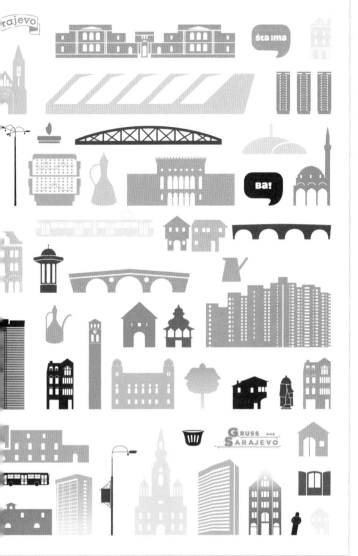

ninadesign.co.ba

Bosnia Herzegovina

Contemporary postcards for a contemporary Sarajevo. Nina Knezevic created a dingbat font for these cards, which feature stylized shapes of traditional Sarajevo establishments such as City Hall, Sebil and Ali Pasha's Mosque, and sights such as street lights, pumpkin seeds, city trams, trash cans, labels from old postcards and titles in Arabic, Cyrillic and Latin. The project marries old with new, visually translating antique picture postcards into fresh vector images.

Remco Schuurbiers

remcoschuurbiers.com

Germany

Urban Desert is the fourth postcard series by multi-disciplinary artist and independent curator Remco Schuurbiers. Born in the Netherlands, Schuurbiers lives and works in Berlin.

Artpostale

Design: Christiane Freilinger

and Yvonne Feldmann

artpostale.com

France and Germany

The name 'Artpostale' is a pun on the French word for postcard, *carte postale*. Yvonne lives and works in Paris and Christiane is based in Hamburg. Atelier Freilinger & Feldmann and Artpostale are active in both France and Germany.

This Alphabet series of 26 postcards was designed by Atelier Freilinger & Feldmann. Sister company Artpostale focuses on postcard projects, and regularly releases postcards produced by Atelier Freilinger & Feldmann from a silkscreen workshop in Hamburg.

Jeff Knowles

mosjef.com

United Kingdom

Jeff Knowles studied graphic design at the University of Salford before joining Research Studios London in 1998. Knowles' photographs for independent studio projects, and Font Shop's fStop Images feature a collection of his work online. The series shown here was created using vector lines.

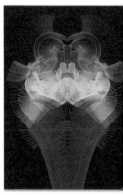

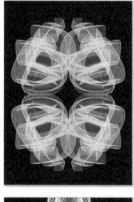

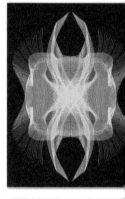

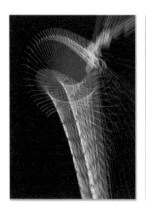

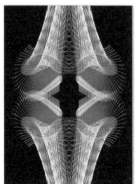

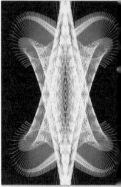

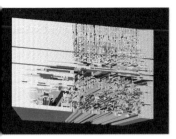

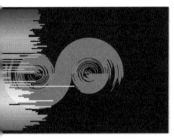

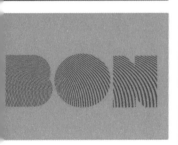

Ben Reece

benreece.com

United Kingdom

Ben Reece studied Graphic Design at Parsons School of Design in New York, and Illustration at London College of Printing and Universität der Künste in Berlin. When not working as a freelancer, Reece works for Neville Brody's Research Studios in London and Paris.

Far left: *Extrude* and *Spectrum* both feature waveforms from a John Chantler song mapped into bands of frequency. *Skyscraper* is a stylized photograph of light reflections connecting two separate buildings. *Bon, Bon* is a visual experiment, as is *Form*, whose simple vectors create an organic form on the card.

Left: *Camo* is a detail inspired by oil patterns in puddles. *Bored* delineates the patterns in fields from the viewpoint of a plane. *JH* is another artistic expression of music – this time Jimi Hendrix setting fire to his guitar.

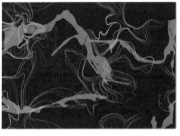

Stylorouge

stylorouge.co.uk

United Kingdom

A set of promotional postcards to celebrate Stylorouge's 25th anniversary. Artworks feature selected images created by Stylorouge from 1981–2006.

Brighten the Corners

Design and Art Direction:

Billy Kiossoglou and Frank Philippin

Client: Goethe Institut, DAAD

brightenthecorners.com

Germany and United Kingdom

London and Stuttgart-based studio Brighten the Corners created the 'Learn German' postcard and poster campaign to promote the German language in British schools and universities. The postcards' use of bold, upper-case typography mirrors the participation of the British tabloid press in the perpetuation of German stereotypes.

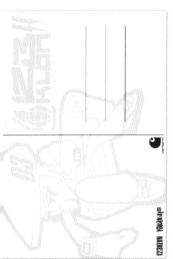

Design: Klor and Scien

123klan.com

Canada

This selection of postcards was used to promote a 123Klan exhibition at the Kitchen93 gallery in Paris.

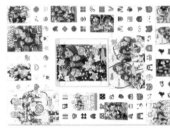

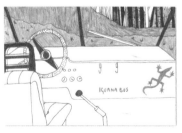

Claire Turner and
George Hadley

claireturner79@yahoo.com

george@cdt-design.co.uk

United Kingdom

A Year in Postcards is a project by Claire Turner and George Hadley who spent a year travelling and working in 13 countries. Each week's adventures are documented in postcards which the travellers then sent home to their families. Drawings, collages, photographs and writing capture the excitement of foreign lands – from Inca ruins to Japanese photo booths. Remarkably all but two of the 104 postcards made it to their final destinations.

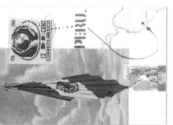

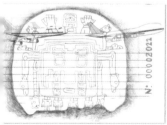

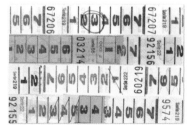

Fabien Barral at Mediafix

Client: Ville de Clermont-Ferrand

fabienbarral.com

mediafix.net

France

The postcard series *Les journées du patalmolne* features eight monumental sculptures in and around the city of Clermont-Ferrand. The monuments are open to the general public as part of a special guided tour. Fabien Barral is art director at design agency Mediafix, also based in Clermont-Ferrand.

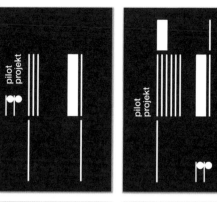

satellitesmistakenforstars.com

Austria and Italy

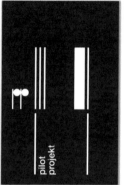

Pilotprojekt is a design gallery space conceived of in order to link creative artists with the design industry. The gallery also acts as a platform for the development of strategies to accommodate the dynamic and fast changing market. Italian graphic designer Alexander Egger developed Pilotprojekt's corporate identity – a visual system featuring two lines and two circles which form the letters 'PP'.

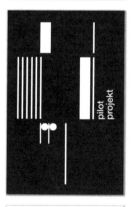
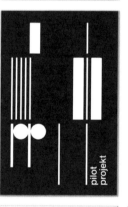

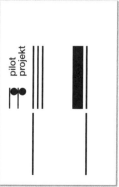

unsteady and easy
marketing target /
www.satellites
mistakenforstars.
com

embarrassed about
overweight sado-
maso housewifes /
www.satellites
mistakenforstars.
com

tired of teenage
hip-hop bitches /
www.satellites
mistakenforstars.
com

depressed by repre-
sentative politics /
www.satellites
mistakenforstars.
com

Alexander Egger

satellitesmistakenforstars.com

Austria and Italy

Above: Self-promotional postcards
for Alexander Egger. Both front
and back are shown.

Right: Postcards accompanying
the launch of limited-edition zines
published by Alexander Egger.
Every zine launch is accompanied
by the distribution of a series of
A5 postcards featuring the cover
image of the zine to friends,
curators, artists and supporters.

A lot of people would
never fall in love
if they didn't hear so
much about it

BUILDINGS, NOT HOMES

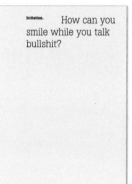

Irritation. How can you
smile while you talk
bullshit?

*In the
long term
we are
all dead*

The top is____
just the____
____bottom
in reverse

people who make noise
are dangerous

Struggling with anger problems or
psychic pain?

places
go, peopl
to see, th
to do

The top is
just the
bottom
in reverse

NOTES ON UNEXPECTED
FEELINGS AFTER
THE RESUMPTION OF
BODILY RELATIONS

but the
sun likes
me

sub/kutan

The top is
just the
bottom
in reverse

Tabas

Design: Cédric Malo

Client: European Parliament

tabas.fr

France

Set of ten postcards featuring handmade typographic illustrations for the Information Office of the European Parliament in Marseille.

Illustration: Tom Gauld

Design: Brighten the Corners

cabanonpress.com

United Kingdom

Robots, Monsters, Etc., a 16-postcard series by London-based Tom Gauld draws on characters such as robots, monsters, dinosaurs, ghosts, astronauts, cavemen... and even a giant floating head.

Atelier Télescopique

ateliertelescopique.com

calacalacity.fr

France

Lille-based Atelier Télescopique developed Calacalacity, an interactive application enabling people to design a house within an imaginary Indian city. The resulting visuals were presented from October 2006 to January 2007 in an exhibition of the same name, which took place at the Maison de l'architecture et de la Ville in Lille, France. Shown here are some of the numerous postcards promoting the Calacalacity exhibition.

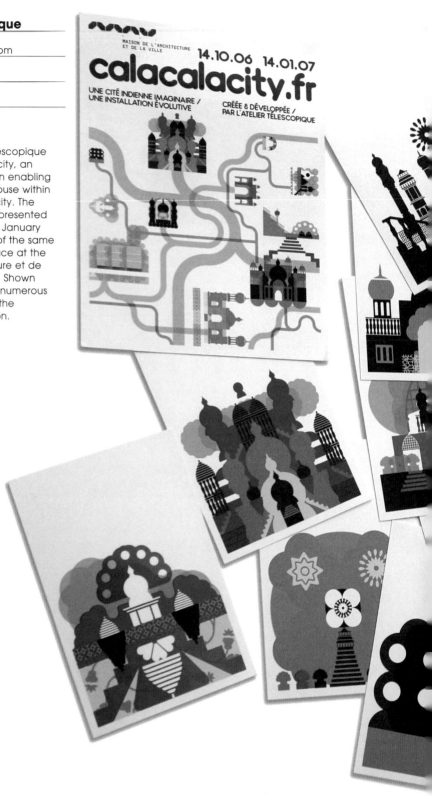

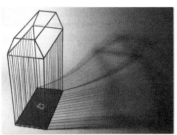

Elisabeth Lecourt

elisabethlecourt.com

United Kingdom

This postcard series features 12 artworks from French artist Elisabeth Lecourt's body of work. Her installations, embroidered handkerchiefs and gloves, paintings and ongoing series of *Les Robes Géographiques* – paper shirts, dresses and other clothes made from folded maps – have been featured in numerous books, newspapers and magazines from around the world.

Daniel Eatock

eatock.com

United Kingdom

With this limited edition set,
Eatock plays with the traditional
conventions of the back of a
postcard's composition,
producing opposite and mirror-
image designs and altered
layouts for big and small
addresses and messages.

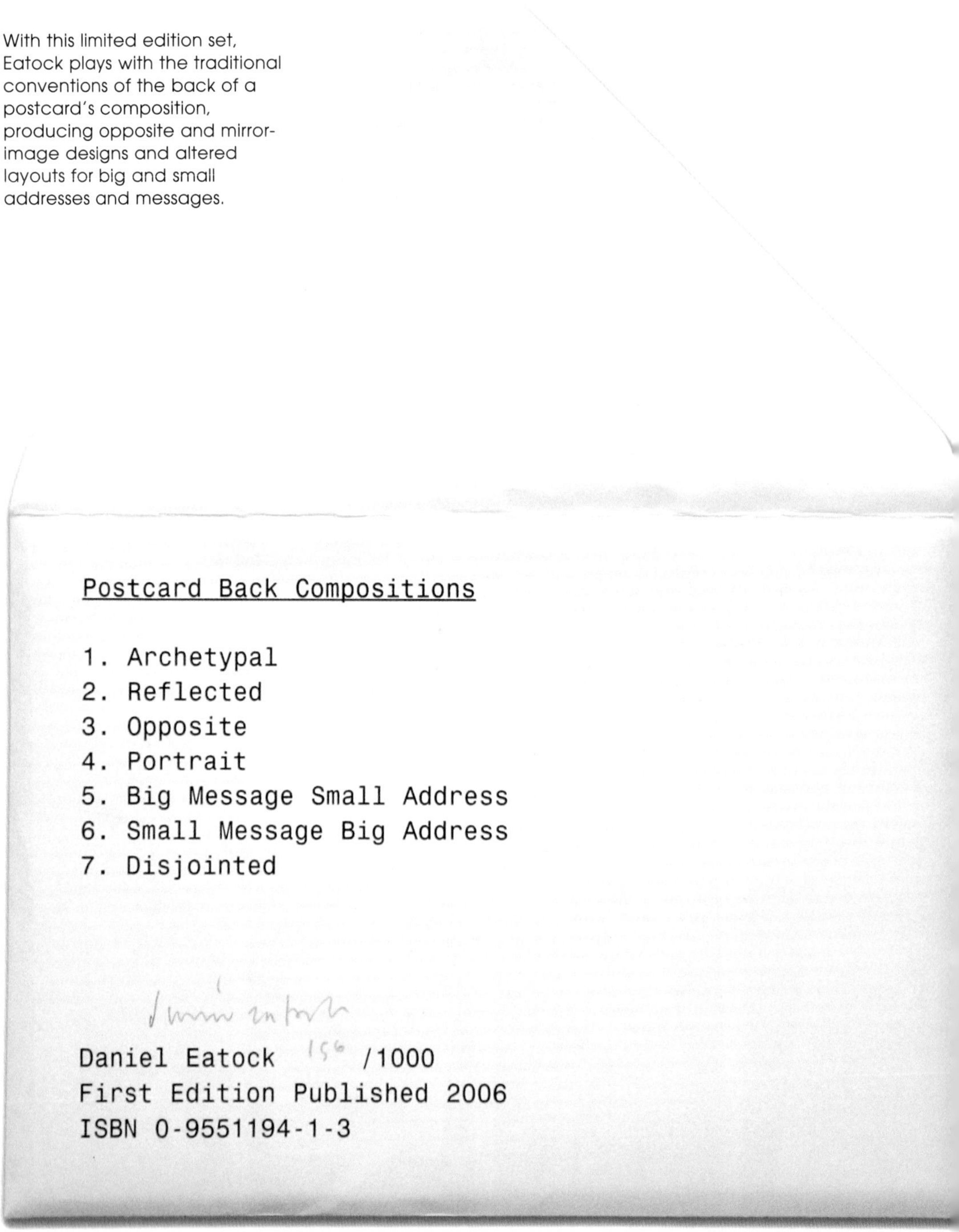

Postcard Back Compositions

1. Archetypal
2. Reflected
3. Opposite
4. Portrait
5. Big Message Small Address
6. Small Message Big Address
7. Disjointed

Daniel Eatock 156 /1000
First Edition Published 2006
ISBN 0-9551194-1-3

Email

Daniel Eatock

eatock.com

United Kingdom

This postcard is temporarily out of stock

Junk Mail

PRIVATE AND CONFIDENTIAL

Email (top) was published in 2002; the other postcards featured here (right) were released in 2004.

Client: Channel Four Television

eatock.com

United Kingdom

The World's Largest Signed and Numbered Limited Edition artwork was published in 2002 when Daniel Eatock was working as a partner at his former company, Foundation 33. Ten team members were authorized to sign and number each postcard.

THE WORLD'S LARGEST SIGNED AND NUMBERED
LIMITED EDITION ARTWORK

September 2002 © Foundation 33

Made for The Art Show, a new ten part series on
Channel 4. Starts Friday 27 September with a
Photography Weekend.

4

This artwork is exclusive for a million people.
The Art Show is inclusive for everybody.

Commissioned by Channel Four Television
Hosted by whitechapel

Distributed by boomerang

The world's largest
signed and numbered
limited edition artwork

Authorised signatory

Your number is

99984

/ One million

Daniel Eatock, Sam Solhaug, Hanna Werning, Lyn Winter, Flávia Müller Medeiros,
Mark Hopkins, Soo Hong, Miles Caro, Naoko Sato, Kirsty Carter

The world's largest
signed and numbered
limited edition artwork

Authorised signatory

Your number is

99985

/ One million

Daniel Eatock, Sam Solhaug, Hanna Werning, Lyn Winter, Flávia Müller Medeiros,
Mark Hopkins, Soo Hong, Miles Caro, Naoko Sato, Kirsty Carter

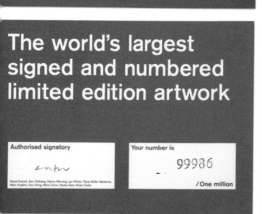

The world's largest
signed and numbered
limited edition artwork

Authorised signatory

Your number is

99986

/ One million

Daniel Eatock, Sam Solhaug, Hanna Werning, Lyn Winter, Flávia Müller Medeiros,
Mark Hopkins, Soo Hong, Miles Caro, Naoko Sato, Kirsty Carter

The world's largest
signed and numbered
limited edition artwork

Authorised signatory

Your number is

99987

/ One million

Daniel Eatock, Sam Solhaug, Hanna Werning, Lyn Winter, Flávia Müller Medeiros,
Mark Hopkins, Soo Hong, Miles Caro, Naoko Sato, Kirsty Carter

1201am

Design: Laurie Forehand

1201am.com

USA

Based in Atlanta, Georgia, 1201am is both a design brand and product line by graphic designer Laurie Forehand. Forehand provides contemporary creative solutions for textiles, fashion and housewares, working in printed matter and digital, interactive and web media. The collection of eight postcard designs shown here is called Postal Decorativ.

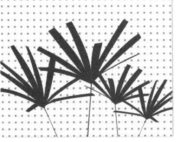

I meant what I said.

There's something you should know.

I know in my heart that you lied.

Design: Alison Riley

seteditions.com

USA

Set Editions was founded in 2004 and is owned by Alison Riley, who is also responsible for the company's clean design. A range of postcards made from recycled and post-consumer materials, the line includes these foil stamped postcards (left) made from 100% recycled chipboard.

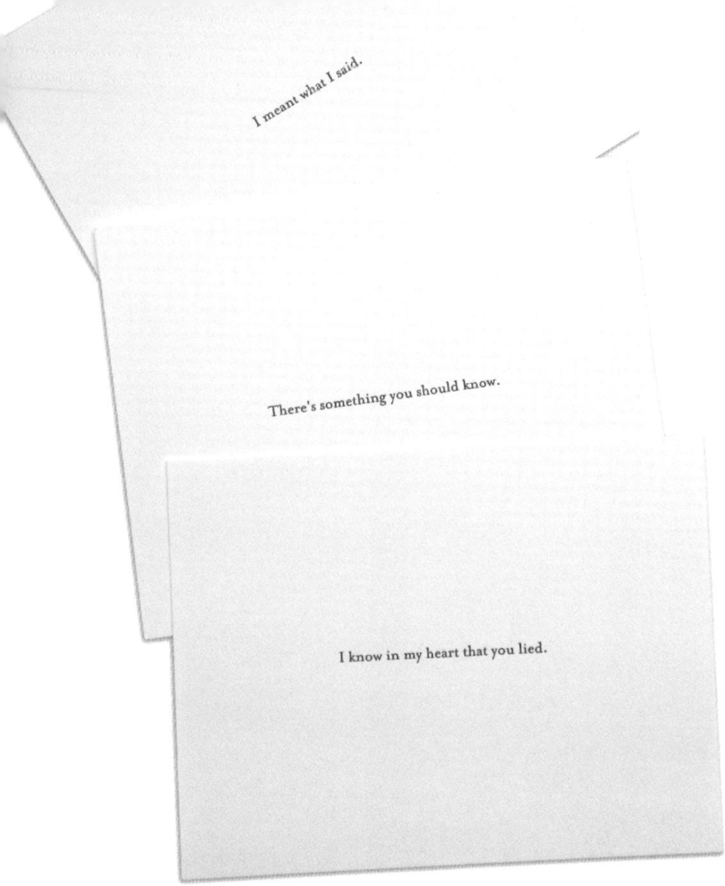

Date: _____

Time: _____

Location: _____

WWW.SETEDITIONS.COM

NOTTINGHAM
TRENT UNIVERSITY
ART & DESIGN
DEGREE SHOWS 2007
PRIVATE VIEW

NOTTINGHAM
TRENT UNIVERSITY

Un.titled

Client: Nottingham Trent University

un.titled.co.uk

United Kingdom

A special limited-edition set of commemorative postcards made by creative agency Un.titled for the Nottingham Trent University of Art and Design in 2007. The stylistic effect of each card is achieved using foiling (for the front image) and silver screenprinting (back image). Colorplan-textured paper by GFSmith is used for each card, with black card indicating under-graduate work and white card MA-level work.

Studio Output

Design: Steve Payne, Sara Oakley,

Dan Moore, Lydia Lapinski

and Rob Coke

studio-output.com

United Kingdom

Promotional postcards by
Nottingham-based Studio Output,
featuring highlights of their
2003 – 2006 portfolio for clients
such as Ascot, Ministry of Sound,
Tea Factory Bar & Kitchen, The
River, Lizard Lounge, Brass Monkey,
Technique Recordings, Geisha,
DJ Magazine and BBC's 1Xtra.

Graphic design
and art direction for

Arts Council England. Ascot.
BBC Radio 1. Coca-Cola.
Channel 4. The Future
Laboratory. Ministry of Sound.

Graphic design
and art direction

Studio Output™

Studio Output™

Graphic design
and art direction
for retail and leisure

Armada

Creative Direction:

Marko Miladinović

Art Direction:

Darko Miladinović

Photography: Julij Kovačič

armada.si

Slovenia

These postcards were created in 2006 as a promotional set by Ljubljana-based design studio Armada. The nostalgic pictures were derived from old slides found in the artists' attic.

Design: James Brown

generalpattern.net

United Kingdom

This postcard set features artworks created by James Brown, who works together with Jim Laurence in their London-based illustration studio General Pattern.

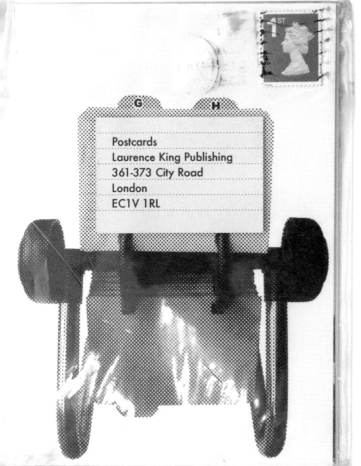

Postcards
Laurence King Publishing
361-373 City Road
London
EC1V 1RL

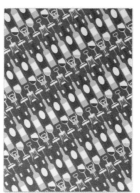

Polite Cards

Illustration: David Shrigley

politecards.com

davidshrigley.com

United Kingdom

David Shrigley's box set of Postcards For Writing On was produced by independent UK publishing company Polite Cards.

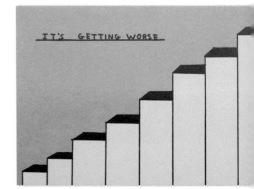

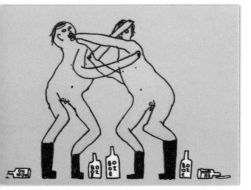

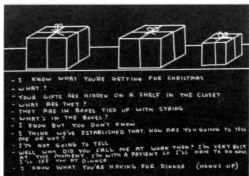

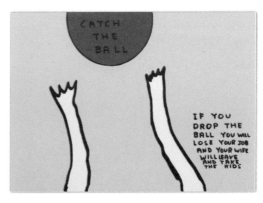

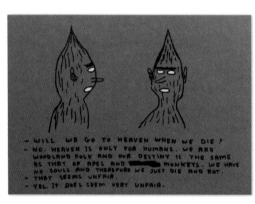

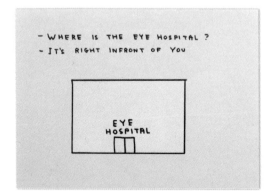

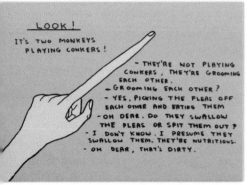

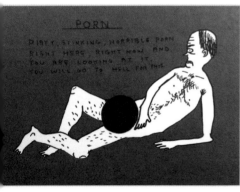

FL@33

Design: Agathe Jacquillat and

Tomi Vollauschek

Client: Friends of the Earth (FoE)

Creative Direction at FoE:

Martha Sakellariou

flat33.com

United Kingdom

This perforated concertina set of eight postcards was designed as part of Friends of the Earth's 2006 The Big Ask campaign. FL@33 was commissioned to illustrate 15 climate change solutions and apply the illustrations across a variety of media, including the cards featured here. All artworks are printed on uncoated and recycled stock.

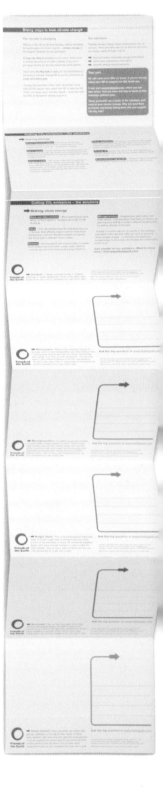

Design: Richard Hart

Photography: Dave Southwood

disturbance.co.za

South Africa

After six years in the same building, Disturbance design studio moved into a new studio space in Durban, South Africa. The studio used a little postcard mailer to advertise their move. The finished piece, a six-panel concertina fold declared, *'We're moving out'*. Once opened, the card reveals a visual pun: staff working at their desks – in the middle of different open urban settings.

2Fresh

2fresh.com

France and Turkey

PXL – Communicating Pixels is a postcard set by design studio 2Fresh. With their 8-bit pixel icons, the uncluttered postcards function as instant message tools – inviting users to contribute to the design by adapting the icons with personalized messages.

Christel Boertjes

christelboertjes.nl

The Netherlands

This postcard set is an excerpt from *Rose Marie* – a photographic portrait by Dutch photographer Christel Boertjes. Christel was selected as one of the Dutch artists of the seventh Pépinières Européennes pour Jeunes Artistes – an artist-in-residence programme. She was working at the Centre Méditeranéen de la Photographie in 2006 on the island of Corsica when she met Rose Marie, a homeless woman.

'For weeks I had seen her walking with her cart, full of rubbish, dolls and books. Rose Marie lived on the streets of Bastia for the past ten years. After a first staged introduction, I would often walk down her street. One night Rose Marie saw me walk by and shouted: "Christelle". I did not have the nerve to tell her I wanted to portray her. That night she carried my camera mount while I shot her surroundings. I hardly speak any French and she no Dutch, we were silent. She asked me for some personal items and clothes, so she could make me a doll.'

Pascal Colrat

pascalcolrat.fr

France

Paris-based graphic artist Pascal Colrat started his series Lost and Found (and Lost Again) in 2003 with images of a tiger, a pigeon and a cat. In 2004 another dimension was added to the project when he created *Lost My Dog Again* and *Found My Teddy*, which were both displayed on huge billboards as part of the Art Grandeur Nature – Signes Extérieurs exhibition at the Biennale d'art contemporaire in Seine-Saint-Denis.

Pascal Colrat

pascalcolrat.fr

France

Postcards from Matoutou Falaise, a series of installations Pascal Colrat created and shot in the Antilles in 2005. The postcard series was created in collaboration with the Bibliothèque de Plaine Commune Aubervilliers.

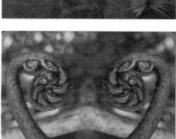

Below (from top to bottom):
Artworks by Dominik Bulka, Tuan
Phan, Yvonne Cheng, Desha
Beamer and Webstellung.

Work created by
SAMIA SALEEM
Seattle, WA
samia@degreesnola.com
www.samiasaleem.com
www.degreesnola.com

Born and raised in New Orleans,
Samia was displaced by Katrina
to Seattle where she currently
resides. *Degrees of Separation*,
which Samia founded, has served
as an outlet for her to share her
thoughts with others who were
affected by the hurricane.

hope.

Work created by SAMIA SALEEM www.samiasaleem.com & www.degreesnola.com

Samia Saleem

Project: Degrees of Separation

degreesnola.com

samiasaleem.com

USA

The postcard book *Degrees of
Separation* features work by
24 designers and artists who were
affected by Hurricane Katrina.
Contributors, who have either
relocated or returned to their
homes, all express their personal
experience of the disaster in
their respective lives. Founded
in 2005, Degrees of Separation
began when Samia Saleem,
herself displaced by the storm,
began collecting postcards. For
many of the featured artists,
design presents a good alternative
to words in expressing the
devastation of the hurricane. A
limited-edition postcard book
with a print run of 750 copies, it
includes 33 full-colour, detachable
postcards and the book itself fits
neatly into a customized sleeve.
Five percent of sale profits are
donated to the AIGA New Orleans
Design Educational Fund.

Below (from top to bottom):
Artworks by Dominik Bulka, Melanie
J. Carnsew, Daniela Marx, Nessim
Higson and Kristy Caldwell.

Below (from top to bottom):
Artworks by Jeff Pastorek, Melanie
J. Carnsew, Mark Kirkpatrick,
Samia Saleem and Yvonne Cheng.

Below (from top to bottom):
Artworks by Tiffany Dantin, Daniela
Marx, Kenneth Robin, Christopher
Palazzo and Lori Ann Reed.

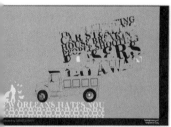

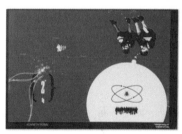

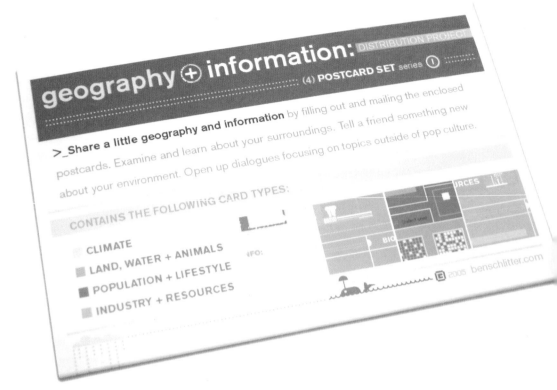

Studiobenben

Project: Geo + Info

Design: Ben Schlitter

geoandinfo.com

benschlitter.com

USA

contribute to – and experience – a fresh way of sharing information. The four cards allow participants to write, draw or scribble details about local climate, land, water, wildlife, population and lifestyle, industry and resources. Schlitter invites participants to submit scans of completed cards to be compiled and launched on an online gallery.

Ben Schlitter of Studiobenben launched the self-initiated Geography and Information Distribution Project. The project consists of four carefully-crafted postcards designed specifically to share geographical details. The cards invite the public to

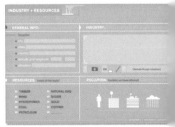

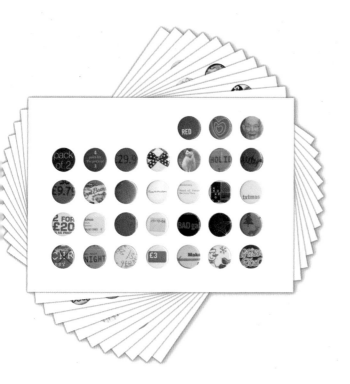

Georgina Potier

georginapotier.com

United Kingdom

Part of a 12-card set by London-based illustrator and designer Georgina Potier, these postcards feature extracts from *Badge a Day for a Year*, the artist's button badge journal project from 2006.

Shown here:
December (left); below, clockwise from top left: January, February, April, March

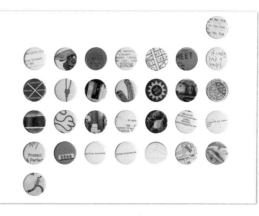

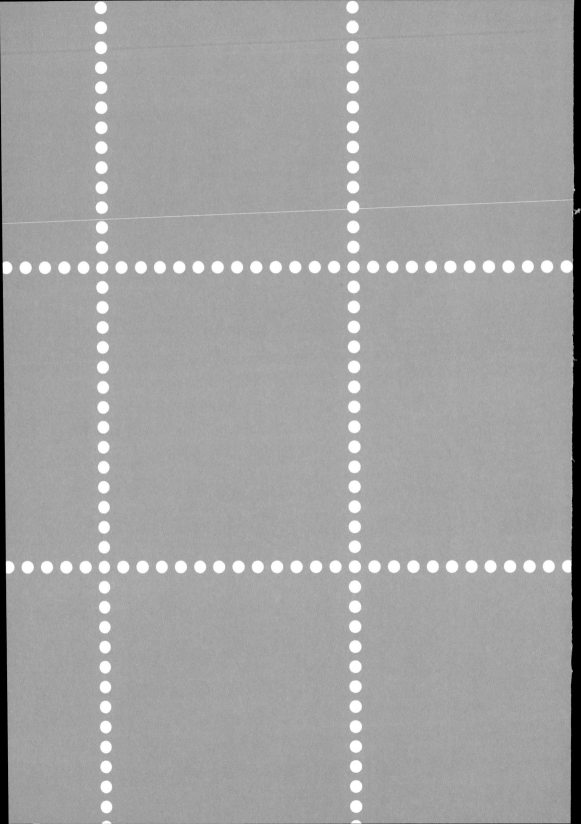

ONGOING PROJECTS

The ongoing projects featured here
include London's annual Royal
College of Art exhibition (RCA
Secret) and the hugely popular
PostSecret project by Frank Warren,
which started as an internet blog
and now includes several bestselling
books. Some of the projects are
interactive, and welcome you to
contribute to them.

1.95

Royal College of Art

Event: RCA Secret

rca.ac.uk

United Kingdom

Initiated by a student in 1994, RCA Secret is a fundraising sale whose profits support the Royal College of Art Fine Art students. In its first 14 years, the exhibition helped to raise over £1 million (US $2 million) to help support emerging artists.

Each year hundreds of artists and designers are asked to create a postcard-sized artwork for the exhibition. Artworks are then displayed at the RCA for one week in November and subsequently sold to the public for £40 (US $80) per piece during two allocated sale days. The 'secret' behind the concept is the actual identity of the artist – each postcard is identified by a number and not by its artist. Postcards are however signed on the back, so would-be buyers have to wait until they've paid for their artwork before they can identify the artist of the work.

The event attracts submissions by artists from all over the world – some are by RCA graduates, current students and staff, others are by renowned contemporary artists including Damien Hirst, David Hockney, Sir Peter Blake, Olafur Eliasson, Tracey Emin, Paula Rego, Christo and David Bailey. Other contributors include fashion designers such as Sir Paul Smith, Julien Macdonald and Manolo Blahnik and film makers such as Terry Gilliam and Ken Loach.

Musicians Graham Coxon (Blur) and John Squire (Stone Roses), who are also practising artists, have contributed. In 2006 the event had over 2,500 postcards.

The Royal College of Art is the world's only entirely postgraduate university of art and design, specializing in teaching and research and offering MA, MPhil and PhD degrees across disciplines such as fine art, applied art, design, communications and humanities. There are over 800 students, and more than 100 professionals on staff, including scholars, leading practitioners of art and design, specialist advisors and distinguished visitors.

janvonholleben.com

Germany

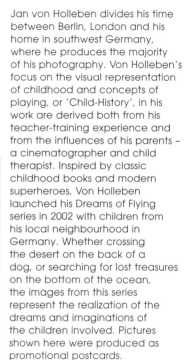

Jan von Holleben divides his time between Berlin, London and his home in southwest Germany, where he produces the majority of his photography. Von Holleben's focus on the visual representation of childhood and concepts of playing, or 'Child-History', in his work are derived both from his teacher-training experience and from the influences of his parents – a cinematographer and child therapist. Inspired by classic childhood books and modern superheroes, Von Holleben launched his Dreams of Flying series in 2002 with children from his local neighbourhood in Germany. Whether crossing the desert on the back of a dog, or searching for lost treasures on the bottom of the ocean, the images from this series represent the realization of the dreams and imaginations of the children involved. Pictures shown here were produced as promotional postcards.

ANIMAL LOVING BRITAIN

BANK HOLIDAY BRITAIN

CHICKEN IN A BUN & CHIPS & COKE

BRITISH CUISINE

£1·50 SENIOR CITIZEN + CHIPS £2·70

BRITISH WILDLIFE

PRIVATE PROPERTY

PRIVATE NO PUBLIC RIGHT OF WAY

Rural Britain

WEIGHT LOSS

Great Britain

MAKE TEA NOT WAR

The News LITTLE MISS CRIMEWAVE JAILED

CHIPS CHIPS Chips

SWINDON it's magic !

The Great British Picnic

Design: Jan Williams

and Chris Teasdale

thecaravangallery.co.uk

United Kingdom

The Caravan Gallery is a mobile exhibition venue and visual arts project run by artists. The project is run by Jan Williams and Chris Teasdale, whose artistic focus is to record the ordinary and extra-ordinary details of life in twenty-first century Britain. Eager to examine clichés and cultural trends, the duo are particularly drawn to the absurd anomalies and curious juxtapositions that are typical of places in transition. The appeal of the resulting postcards lies not in a picturesque aesthetic, but in the celebration of the familiar details that make-up the reality – and surreality – of contemporary Britain.

As Jan and Chris say: *'Unexpected delights are to be found in the most unpromising situations – and, of course, the reverse is true.'*

The Caravan Gallery exhibits at an eclectic range of locations, rural, urban and suburban, from small-scale community events to major festivals and venues.

I'm forced to carry your secret because you were too weak to keep it to yourself.

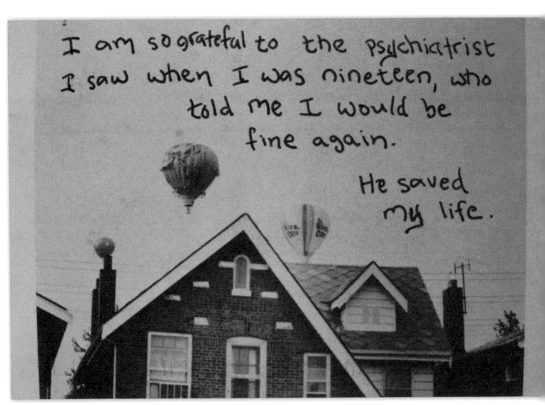

I am so grateful to the psychiatrist I saw when I was nineteen, who told me I would be fine again.

He saved my life.

PostSecret.com

USA

PostSecret began with an idea Frank Warren had for a community art project. Warren printed 3,000 self-addressed postcards and distributed them in public spaces, asking people to write down a secret that had never been revealed and mail it to him anonymously. The response was overwhelming. The secrets were both provocative and profound, and the cards, works of art – carefully constructed by hand. The ever-growing collection of over 100,000 postcards is available online, in four bestselling books and at two travelling art exhibitions.

Weak (opposite page, top), is from his second book *My Secret: A PostSecret book.*

Saved (opposite page, bottom)

Ticket (left, top), *Recycling* (left, second from top) and *Poetry* (left, third from top) are from Warren's first book *PostSecret: Extraordinary Confessions from Ordinary Lives*, *Doctor* (left, bottom)

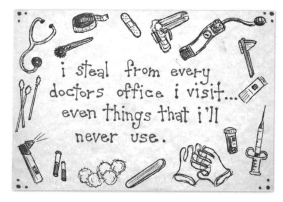

Love to Post

lovetopost.co.uk

United Kingdom

Love to Post (LTP) is a postcard project initiated by UK-based design student Martin Rimmer, in which artists from around the UK are invited to create art with a blank – stamped – postcard. The card is then sent back to Rimmer, who displays it on the project website. Positive feedback on LTP has extended the project to people from around the world – who are willing to pay the postage for their artworks themselves – thus launching the international facet of the project. Postcards shown here are just a few examples of the growing collection.

Opposite: *Anna Hamilton, Carl Murphy, Peskimo, Tado, Lunartik, Al Murphy, Choowi, Jon Burgerman.*

Left (clockwise from top): *Andy Smith, Joan Rimmer, Martin Rimmer.*

Allistair J. Burt

Project: Small World Experiment

smallworldexperiment.com

United Kingdom

This postcard (above) is part of an experiment exploring the Milgram, or small-world, phenomenon in which all strangers are linked through six degrees of separation. At the project's outset, fifty-four little boxes were released to strangers around the world, each box containing a jigsaw piece. The aim is that the boxes will be returned to their owner Allistair J. Burt, who works in an architect's office in Glasgow. When returned, the jigsaw pieces will be reassembled and mounted on display. The only rule governing the experiment is that each person can only pass the box on to someone that they personally know. Thus the boxes travel from friend to friend and from country to country. As a way of tracking the route that each package takes, a series of pre-addressed postcards were included. Each person was asked to complete a few questions then pop the postcard into the post. Returned cards are then used to plot the journeys of the packages online.

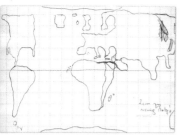
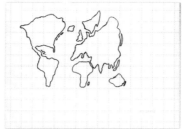

Joana Niemeyer

Project: My World

joananiemeyer.com

United Kingdom

Joana Niemeyer's project My World explores people's memory of the world map. Postcards sent to various people around the world are returned completed with the recipient's individual hand-drawn rendition of the world map. Some of the results are shown here. The bottom two images show Stefan Sagmeister's response.

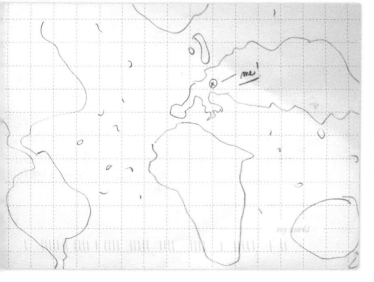

CONTRIBUTOR PROFILES

2.09

1201am
1201am.com
Laurie Forehand is a graphic designer currently working in Atlanta, Georgia. As a New Year's goal in January 2000, Laurie began the online design studio and brand 1201am. Focusing on innovation in design, the site showcases online projects and digital artwork created by talented designers from around the globe. The site is an open area for artists to display their work and for industry trends and information to be shared. In recent years, 1201am has featured a new line of paper goods and housewares which feature Laurie's signature design style. She also has a line of rugs and wall coverings in the works for release in 2008.

123Klan
123klan.com
Scien and Klor have been graffiti artists since 1989. 123Klan were the first to blend graffiti writing and graphic art on the web, making it not just an exhibition tool but a new creative medium. For these trailblazers, graffiti writing and graphic art are closely linked and, as they say themselves, `style is the message'. Their monograph was published in 2004 and an updated version was released in 2007 by French publisher Pyramyd Editions.

2Fresh
2fresh.com
2Fresh provides its clients with creative communication design solutions for the new communication era. They offer professional design services in the areas of interactive, motion graphics and static design. Founded in 2003 in the USA, 2Fresh's European base operates from Paris and Istanbul. International clients include Corona Extra, Snickers, Vodafone, Wincor-Nixdorf, Bogazici University, Galatasaray University, Hillside SU Hotel, Kemer Group and Selga. Their work has been featured in numerous books and magazines around the world.

A

A2 Design
a2design.co.uk
Specializing in branding, corporate identity, web design, corporate and sales literature, Graphic design consultancy A2 Design was founded in 2000 by Andrew Pengilly. Prior to starting up A2, Pengilly worked with international design consultancies, including Pentagram in London and Carré Noir in Paris, where he was creative director. Pengilly has won numerous creative awards and has judged the prestigious D&AD annual awards. A2 is based in Twickenham, Middlesex, UK.

Mark Adams
markadamsimages.com
Mark Adams is an RCA graduate and photographic artist. A freelance photographer for the past ten years, the focus of his work ranges from street photography to colour landscape photography. He has exhibited in the United States and England and is represented by Millennium Images.

Airside
airside.co.uk
Founded in 1999, Airside is a London-based design company. The people of Airside come from different disciplines, ranging from computer programming and English literature to textiles and graphic design, as well as clubs and music. Enjoyment and passion are the prerequisites behind all Airside's work – be it websites, animation, T-shirts or CD sleeves.

Marcela Alejandra
marcelaalejandra.com
Born in Chile, Marcela Alejandra arrived in Sweden in the early Eighties. Marcela developed a love of books, writing and drawing while growing up in the highrises of suburban Stockholm. She obtained her Bachelor's degree in Illustration at London's Camberwell College of Arts in 2004, and MA from the Royal College of Art. `I am fascinated by the stories of "ordinary" people and everyday life. I am particularly drawn to the darker aspect of memory and imagination, and in the potential for cruelty and beauty in people, in our experiences and in our environment.'

April-Mediengruppe
april-mg.de
Karin Kloubert was born in Romania and raised in Turkey and Germany. She studied in Germany at the Fachhoch schule Trier and at London's Camberwell College of Art before moving to Berlin in 2000. Kloubert is working as a freelance graphic designer and, since 2005, as a founding member of April-Mediengruppe.

Nutre Arayavanish
nutrejeweller.com
In summer 2007 Nutre Arayavanish obtained her Master's degree from the Royal College of Art in London. Arayavanish has received numerous prestigious awards, including the Theo Fennel Excellence in Jewellery award at the RCA, Student Designer of the Year at the 2007 UK Jewellery Awards from the British Jewellers' Association and was New Designer of The Year at the New Designers Exhibition, held at London's Design Business Centre.

Armada
armada.si
Armada is a graphic design studio based in Ljubljana, Slovenia, which develops brand concepts and interior design. Their logo for 'Halo Safet' was selected for a Best of Nation award by Eulda – the European Logo Design Annual 2007 – as the most innovative idea from Slovenia. Armada's clients include Pat Airways, Human Rights Ombudsman, SiMobil, Baby Centre Shop and Transport TV.

Artiva Design
artiva.it
akeshape.it
danieledebatte.it
Genoa-based studio Artiva Design was founded in 2003 by Daniele De Batté and Davide Sossi. The studio works across many mediums, including web design, illustration, typography, photography and graphic design. De Batté and Sossi also work on independent projects including their patterns collection, akeshape.it.

Artpostale
rtpostale.com
Christiane Freilinger and Yvonne Feldmann founded Atelier Freilinger & Feldmann in Hamburg. Both studied Visual Communication at different international colleges before joining forces in 1999. Atelier Freilinger & Feldmann and their sister company and postcard project rtpostale are based both in Germany and Paris.

Atelier Télescopique
ateliertelescopique.com
alacalacity.fr
Atelier Télescopique is a multi-disciplinary graphic design studio. Founded in 1998, the studio works across many areas, including creating typefaces and multimedia applications. The client list is equally diverse – ranging from corporate industries to institutions. The studio is based in Lille, France.

B

Lucas Ballocchi
brocoli.cl
Lucas Ballocchini is a graphic designer born and working in Santiago, Chile. Most of his work is related to street art. He is currently working at Brocoli, a collective of designers dedicated to character design.

Fabien Barral at Mediafix
fabienbarral.com
mediafix.net
Fabien Barral is a freelance photographer and graphic designer based in St Bonnet, France. He is also art director at Mediafix.

BC, MH
bcmh.co.uk
BC,MH is a graphic design studio founded in 2004 by RCA graduates Ben Chatfield and Mark Hopkins. Working for a broad range of clients, BC,MH create work in both 3D and print for publishing, marketing, exhibition, events and brand applications. Projects include exhibition graphics for the Turner Prize Retrospective show at Tate Britain (2007); design of the Turner Prize and British Art publication for Tate Publishing; marketing campaign and exhibition graphics for Jerwood Applied Arts Prize: Jewellery (2007); exhibition graphics and catalogue for the Gothic Nightmares show at Tate Britain (2006); marketing campaign and exhibition graphics for RCA Secret (2006); design of *Housey Housey: A Pattern Book of Ideal Homes*.

Agnese Bicocchi
agnesbic.com
Illustrator Agnese Bicocchi grew up in Italy and moved to London to study visual arts. Since finishing her Illustration degree in 2004, she has created images, books, paintings and artifacts.

Christel Boertjes
christelboertjes.nl
Dutch photographer Christel Boertjes was selected in 2005 as one of the Dutch artists of the seventh Pépinières Européennes pour Jeunes Artistes – an artist-in-residence programme which she undertook in Corsica. More grants and residencies followed, including Skaftfell, Iceland in 2006 and Hirsholmene, Denmark in 2008. Christel regularly exhibits across Europe.

Mr Bowlegs
mrbowlegs.co.uk
Mr Bowlegs is talented 21 year-old designer Jeffrey Bowman. He graduated from the University of Huddersfield, UK, in 2007.

Adam Brickles
superskint.co.uk
Adam Brickles studied at the London College of Printing (now London College of Communication) and graduated in 2003 from Norwich School of Art and Design. In 2007 he obtained a Master's degree in Communication Design from London's Central Saint Martins. Using print, text and imagery, his work examines the similarities between football and religion.

Brighten the Corners
brightenthecorners.com
Billy Kiossoglou and Frank Philippin run Brighten the Corners – an independent, multi-disciplined design and strategy consultancy with offices in London and Stuttgart. Established in 1999, the small organization handles both large and small-scale projects. Whether designing a book, a stamp or branding an organization, their designs focus on clear and direct communication.

Javier González Burgos

illustrationartworks.blogspot.com
javiergbilustraciones.blogspot.com
Javier González grew up in Buenos Aires, Argentina and studied at the Graphic Design and Art College. As a freelance illustrator in Buenos Aires, Javier has illustrated over 40 books. His work has been published in Spain, Chile, Mexico, Colombia, Puerto Rico and the Unites States and exhibited in Sweden, Italy and Japan. His award-winning designs are created digitally, without any preliminary sketches or scanning.

Anthony Burrill

anthonyburrill.com
Anthony Burrill studied Graphic Design at Leeds Polytechnic before completing his Master's degree at the Royal College of Art in London. He works as a freelance designer producing print, moving image and interactive design and his projects include poster campaigns for London Underground, Diesel, Hans Brinker Budget Hotel, Playstation, Nike and interactive web-based projects for Kraftwerk and Air. Anthony lives and works on the Isle of Oxney, Kent.

Allistair J. Burt

smallworldexperiment.com
holeinmypocket.com
Allistair J. Burt studied architecture at Strathclyde University. He formed Hole in my Pocket, an artistic collaborative website. Through Hole in my Pocket, Burt has worked on a range of projects, from designing T-shirts for the IDEAS factory, curating and exhibiting, writing and illustrating a book for Trajectory publishing and directing a short film for Channel 4. He is developing a new show about his ongoing project, the Small World Experiment.

C

Nick Cannons

nickcannons.co.uk
Designer Nick Cannons moved to London after graduating from Surrey Institute of Art and Design (UCCA). Having worked with The District and Mark Smith Design, Cannons opened his own studio working on small print projects for arts-based organizations.

The Caravan Gallery

thecaravangallery.co.uk
The Caravan Gallery is a mobile exhibition venue and visual arts project run by artists Jan Williams and Chris Teasdale. Eager to examine clichés and cultural trends in Britain, the Caravan Gallery exhibits at an eclectic range of locations, rural, urban and suburban, from small-scale community events to major festivals and venues.

Colourbox

colourboxshop.bigcartel.com
Joe Rogers runs illustration and graphic design practice and shop Colourbox, based in Birmingham, UK. Colourbox works in all areas of design and illustration, producing contemporary designs for both national and international editorial, advertising and corporate clients, including French cultural magazine *Standard*, American based *Let Go* magazine and online arts magazine *Iniciativa Colectiva*. Colourbox also produces T-shirt designs for Japan-based retailer Graniph, illustrations on tote bags for French design company LoveBy, and branding for American musician Peter Hadar and 3Sided Photography.

Pascal Colrat

pascalcolrat.fr
Born in 1967, Pascal Colrot graduated from the École Nationale Supérieure des Beaux-Arts de Paris. Pascal is a graphic artist and photographer and works with a wide range of different cultural and political institutions including Amnesty International, Act Up, Le Tarmac de la villette, l'Opéra de Lille, la Scène Nationale de Rouen and le Grand Théâtre de Lorient. In 2002 he exhibited at the Centre Georges Pompidou as part of the exhibition Signes de la Biélorussie. In the same year his monograph was published by Pyramyd Editions.

Concrete Hermit

concretehermit.com
London-based Concrete Hermit was started by Chris Knight in 2004 and has since worked with selected artists to produce graphically-led products including T-shirts, books and badges. Concrete Hermit provides a platform that promotes interesting work with respect to both the artist and the buyer.

D

D-Fuse

dfuse.com
D-Fuse is a collective of London-based artists who explore a wide range of creative media. Working with cutting-edge technology, D-Fuse encourage their audience to reflect on the process of experiencing multi-dimensional, multi-sensory art. Their explorations of live audiovisual performance, mobile media, web, print, art and architecture, TV and film, have been shown internationally at venues and events such as V&A Museum, London, Sonar, Barcelona, Prix Ars Electronica, Linz, Mori Arts Centre, Tokyo, San Francisco Museum of Modern Art, Eyebeam, New York, Mu, Eindhoven, and onedotzero, Rotterdam and Seoul film festivals. The D-Fuse collective has collaborated with musicians such as Beck, classical composer Steve Reich and Italian ensemble Alter Ego. Recent works include the publication of *VJ: Audiovisual Art + VJ Culture*.

Detail. Design Studio

detail.ie
Detail. Design Studio, established in 2004, is a creative design studio operating in Dublin. Specializing in identity, print communications and interactive design, their mantra is *'to blend business and creative criteria to produce good design solutions – remember, good design makes things better.'*

Marion Deuchars
mariondeuchars.com
Marion Deuchars studied Illustration and Printmaking at Duncan of Jordanstone College of Art and the Royal College of Art in 1989. Along with fellow RCA students she formed an art and design studio and continues today to work from a multi-disciplinary studio in North London. Since graduating, Deuchars has worked with major design and advertising agencies worldwide. Her commercial work covers corporate literature, publishing, editorial, packaging, retail, advertising, design for web, brand development, craft, and architecture. She has been a member of AGI (Alliance Graphique International) since 2001.

Marcus Diamond
marcusdiamond.com
Marcus Diamond set up Neasden Control Centre with Steve Smith a few years ago and has worked for clients such as ActionAid, MTV and Playboy. Diamond subsequently moved into freelance work.

Disturbance
disturbance.co.za
Disturbance is a small design studio based in Durban, South Africa. Started 10 years ago by siblings Richard and Susie Hart, a book on their work entitled These are our Favourite Things can be ordered through their website.

DTM_INC
dddesign.nl/dtm/illus.html
boomerang.nl/DTM_INC
Behind the mysterious DTM_INC is part-time graphic designer and illustrator Danny Geerlof. He regularly designs postcards for Boomerang, Netherlands. Danny has revealed that DTM_INC stands for 'Dan Tha Man Incorporated'.

Daniel Eatock
eatock.com
London-based Daniel Eatock's work engages with the connections between image and language. Focusing on conceptual art, he is especially interested in the connection of the start and end points of hand-drawn circles.

eBoy
eboy.com
Berlin-based eBoy was founded in 1998 by Steffen Sauerteig, Svend Smital and Kai Vermehr when they acquired the eBoy.com domain. The basic idea driving eBoy is to embrace the possibilities of the emerging digital world. eBoy's design focus centres around the use of pixels, while their business focus prioritizes freestyle work. Clients include MTV.com, SAP and Adidas.

Alexander Egger
satellitesmistakenforstars.com
Alexander Egger is an italian-born Vienna-based graphic designer who also dabbles in art, writing and music. Working in different media on cultural and commercial projects, his clients include Adidas, Siemens, Designforum, Technisches Museum Wien, BMW, Burda Medien, Sony – Connect Europe, T-Mobile, Futurehouse Vienna, Design Austria, Vienna City Hall, Bundesministerium für Arbeit und Wirtschaft and Austrian Railways (ÖBB). His first monograph Satellites Mistaken for Stars is published by Gingko Press, California.

Elfen
elfen.co.uk
Cardiff-based Elfen is a bilingual design company. Elfen formed in 1997 and comprises a multi-disciplinary team of dedicated and flexible designers. They also acquire and manage print on behalf of clients.

Emily Forgot
emilyforgot.co.uk
Emily Forgot is London-based designer and illustrator Emily Alston. Since graduating from Liverpool School of Art and Design she has worked both independently as well as with various design studios. She is developing her own range of 'forgot' products which are available online and include printed textiles as well as limited-edition prints and ceramics. Clients include Orange, The Guardian, The Telegraph, Dazed and Confused, John Brown, Citrus Publishing, BBC, Fallon, Bang and Olufsen, Vandal and Paul Smith.

Emmi
emmi.co.uk
Originally from Finland, Emmi Salonen graduated from the University of Brighton in 2001 with a Bachelor's degree in Graphic Design. After moving to Italy to work at Fabrica, Benetton's controversial young designers' melting pot, she worked at karlssonwilker in New York, before starting her own practice, Emmi, in London in 2005.

Catalina Estrada
catalinaestrada.com
Catalina Estrada was born and raised in Colombia and has been living in Barcelona since 1999 working in the fields of art, graphic design and illustration. Presented as a fresh and new design talent by Communication Arts and Computer Arts magazines, her work has featured in books by Die Gestalten Verlag, Swindle, DPI, Ppaper and Graphic Magazine. Some of her clients include: Paul Smith, Coca-Cola, Custo-Barcelona, Salomon, Honda, Nike and Chronicle Books.

F

FL@33
flat33.com
See page 224

Fluid
fluidesign.co.uk
meisai.ne.nu
outcrowdcollective.com
From brand identity to advertising campaigns, 3D modelling and exhibitions to packaging and web design – Fluid employs a strategic approach and progressive design style to create a concept that will fulfil any design requirement. Areas of expertise include design, branding, advertising, multimedia and web design. Fluid's art director Lee Basford designed the postcards featured in this book.

Monica Fraile
monica.fraile.free.fr
Freelance graphic designer Monica Fraile lives and works in Paris. In 2000 she obtained a BFA Graphic Design from the School of Visual Arts (SVA), New York City.

G

Geneviève Gauckler
g2works.com
Geneviève Gauckler graduated from the ENSAD (Ecole Nationale Supérieure des Arts Décoratifs) in 1991 in Paris where she lives and works. Geneviève works with simple, colourful shapes to create her trademark characters. Three books have been published about her work, in Japan by Gas Book and in France by Pyramyd. Geneviève is also a member of the experimental video collective Pleix. Clients include Renault, Skype, Bourjois, Coca-Cola and Lane Crawford.

Tom Gauld
cabanonpress.com
RCA graduate Tom Gauld is an illustrator and comic book artist based in London. He has written and illustrated comics *Guardians of the Kingdom*, *Three very small Comics* and *Hunter & Painter* as well as producing comic stories and illustrations for various publications including *The Guardian*, *The Independent* and *The New Yorker*. Gauld runs Cabanon Press with Simone Lia, and together they have created comics *First* and *Second* which were republished as *Both* by Bloomsbury.

General Pattern
generalpattern.net
General Pattern is the London-based illustration studio of Jim Laurence and James Brown. '*Through our strengths in ornamentation and pattern making we produce intelligently-crafted work suited to the individual project, whether it requires lo-fi decorative typography or graphic tessellation.*' General Pattern clients include Rangerover, *The Guardian*, *Waitrose Food Illustrated*, Kula Shaker, *The Telegraph Magazine*, Marks & Spencer, Royal Consort Papers and Paperchase. General Pattern are represented by New Division illustration agency.

Gregory Gilbert-Lodge
gilbert-lodge.com
Gregory Gilbert-Lodge is an award-winning illustrator working mainly for editorial clients. Until 2005 he was a member of Silex – a group of seven artists and illustrators – whose *Silex – My Way* (2000) was published by Die Gestalten Verlag. His work has been exhibited internationally and has also been published in numerous magazines and books. His latest publication, *Two Faced* features his beautiful and striking portraits.

Pilar Gorriz
pilargorriz.com
Barcelona-based studio Pilar Gorriz, Diseño Grafico was launched in 1988. Founder Pilar Gorriz studied at Eina Escola de Disseny i Art and specializes in corporate identities and editorial design projects. She has returned to her college to teach, and also tutors the postgraduate course for Art Direction at the Ramon Llull University. Her body of work has been published in *Select C*, *Select D*, *Select E*, *BCD Selection*, International TypoGraphic Awards 04, *Visual Magazine* and Laus Prizes 29.

Graphic Oil
graphicoil.com
Amsterdam-based design studio Graphic Oil was founded in 2000 and is run by Henk van het Nederend (Lasko) and Chris Visser (Krekel). Starting a studio while still at art academy, they began working with nightclubs in Amsterdam and soon expanded to create websites, visuals for advertising and provide art direction for magazines. After seven years as a multi-disciplinary design studio, the two have focused on developing the craftsmanship of their core business: illustration and typographic design work.

Nazario Graziano
ngdesign.it
Italian graphic designer Nazario Graziano is art director for the Firewater club as well as working as an illustrator for companies such as MTV and Vodafone. Graziano draws, cuts out and collects clippings for his analogue and digital collages. He has also launched several creative platforms for emerging talents including website *Revolver-Lover* and *ANTI Magazine*.

H

Hat-trick
hat-trickdesign.co.uk
The multi-disciplinary, London-based design consultancy Hat-trick was set up in 2001 by Gareth Howat, David Kimpton and Jim Sutherland. The team has since won 50 British Design and Art Direction awards and ten Design Week awards. Clients include Abbey National, D&AD, Brooks Macdonald, Capital Radio, Christian Aid, Dresdner Bank, Dyson, Fairbridge, House of Fraser, Independent Radio News, Land Securities, National Museums of Scotland, Natural History Museum, Neurosurgical Centre (USA), NESTA, Royal Albert Hall, Royal Mail, Somerset House, The Salvation Army, Twickenham Stadium, UBS, Xchanging and Xfm.

Al Heighton
alanheighton.co.uk
Artist, designer and illustrator Al Heighton graduated with a degree in Graphic design from the University of Salford in 2001. Heighton's tools include paint, pen, pencil and computer. He has worked for Images 27, *The Face*, high street chain Schuh and the South Yorkshire Police. Commercial commissions include editorial illustration work for the *Big Issue*, *MYOB* magazine, and *InCirculation* magazine. Heighton has exhibited his work at the Mall Galleries, Truman Brewery, Mantos, Doncaster Art Gallery and Museum, Commonwealth Institute and Sheridan Russel Gallery.

Hellovon
hellovon.com
Hellovon is run by London-based illustrator Von whose work is influenced by music, fashion and design. His work blends traditional and digital mark-making techniques. Since establishing Hellovon at the start of 2006, his work has been exhibited internationally in the London Design Museum, Cosh, Espeis, Exposure, Soma, Triple 5 Soul and Stolen Space galleries. He has also built a client list including 4AD, Ogilvy and Mather, Non-Format, Dazed & Confused, Wallpaper, The New York Times and The Guardian.

Jan von Holleben
janvonholleben.com
Jan von Holleben divides his time between Berlin, London and his home in southwest Germany where he produces the majority of his photography. Following a professional photographic apprenticeship with a commercial photographer, von Holleben moved to England to study at Surrey Institute of Art and Design in Farnham. Following graduation, he established two photographic collectives, became picture editor and photographic director for magazines and agencies and won several prestigious awards for his own photography. Jan von Holleben's work is now widely published and exhibited internationally.

Rod Hunt
rodhunt.com
London-based illustrator Rod Hunt's work draws on humour, retro graphics and contemporary culture. Rod has been been commissioned by an international range of publishing, design and advertising clients. He is the art director for rising rock band The Southern Electrics and deputy chairman of the Association of Illustrators (AOI), which was established in 1973 to advance and protect illustrators' rights and encourage professional standards.

Hush
studio-hush.com
Hush is an urban artist based in the UK. The core of his work is in illustration, stencilling and painting. Following his success with graphic pop-culture illustrations in posters and stencils, Hush has diversified into other areas, including fine art, design and fashion. Hush has worked as a graphic designer and illustrator in London, Edinburgh, Newcastle and Hong Kong, where he worked for a few of the world's leading toy brands. He studied Graphic Design and Illustration at Newcastle School of Art and Design for five years.

I

Iceberg
iceberg.it
Italian-based Iceberg s.r.l. Advertising Agency has been offering services and consultancy in advertising and promotion communication since the early 1980s. The organization is divided into three main branches: Iceberg Advertising, Iceberg Media and Iceberg Design. Iceberg covers advertising campaigns, TV, radio advertisements, packaging, public relations and exhibition design.

Riitta Ikonen
rittaikonen.com
Riitta Ikonen describes herself as an enthusiastic Finn with an interest in most things. She studied Illustration at the University of Brighton, and after working in advertising, decided to pursue a Masters degree in Communication Art and Design at the Royal College of Art in London. She has a passion for collecting and creating things out of obscure findings.

I Make Things
imakethings.co.uk
Inspired by adventures in mountains and forests and the magic of rural Japan, I Make Things, or Andrew Groves, is an illustrator who occasionally creates small objects and beasts. Clients include Foundation Skateboards, Computer Arts Magazine, Die Gestalten Verlag, Pictoplasma, Graniph, CBBC and Sony Ericsson.

Inksurge
inksurge.com
'Brewed' in Manila, Philippines 2002, this design studio, or creative brewery, was concocted by Joyce Tai and Rex Advincula. Steeped in a rich passion for using the visual arts both as a communication tool and a public service, the Inksurge design trademark has gained recognition from the local and international web design, print and interactive scenes. Inksurge brew creative media for web and interactive design, illustration, print, music packaging, apparel, exhibitions and logos.

J

Nicole Jacek
NicoleJacek@aol.com
Nicole Jacek studied at the Freie Kunstschule, Stuttgart and obtained her diploma from the Merz Akademie, Academy of Art and Design, Stuttgart. After serving internships at Springer & Jacoby in Hamburg, Karlssonwilker Inc. and Sagmeister Inc. in New York City, Jacek moved back to Ludwigsburg, Germany, where she now works in her own practice Studio Nicole Jacek.

Jeremyville
jeremyville.com
Jeremyville is an artist, product designer and animator. He wrote and produced the world's first book on designer toys, Vinyl Will Kill, which was published by IdN. In 2007 he participated in a group show at Colette alongside KAWS, Fafi, Futura, Mike Mills and Takashi Murakami and has initiated the 'sketchel' art satchel project. His art has been published in numerous international design books and magazines. Clients include Converse, Rossignol, Colette, Coca-Cola, MTV, Kidrobot, Refill, Graniph, Wooster Collective, Adidas, Artoyz, Domestic Vinyl, Corbis, Red Bull, Pop Cling, 55 DSL and Beck.

Johnson Banks

johnsonbanks.co.uk

Michael Johnson is the author of best-selling design primer *Problem Solved*. Johnson also runs the internationally-renowned design company, johnson banks, which produces brand and identity schemes for clients as varied as the British Government, Shelter, Christian Aid, More Th>n and the British Film Institute. The small company also operates in France, USA and Japan. Banks has won several design awards and has two dozen posters in the permanent collection of the V&A. He co-curated the Rewind Exhibition at the V&A in 2002–3, was D&AD's president in 2003 and held the first solo exhibition of his design work in Ginza, Tokyo, in 2004.

Juju's Delivery

jujus-delivery.com

Juju's Delivery was founded by Berlin-based artist Julia Schonlau. Following a degree in Media Art at Chelsea College in London, Schonlau began her career designing covers, flyers and posters for musician friends. She has since collaborated with Rojo, Pictoplasma, MTV and Mercedes Benz, and published drawings in various magazines. Her work has been exhibited in New York's Cinder's Gallery, Colette in Paris and throughout Berlin. Julia's drawings have been applied to skateboards, belts, cars and walls. Her first book *The Dead, the Damned and the Children of the Revolution* was released by Spanish Rojo Editions and quickly sold out.

K

Kapitza

kapitza.com
kapitza.com/shop

Kapitza is a design partnership that formed in London between sisters Petra Kapitza and Nicole Kapitza. Originally from southern Germany, the sisters have been living and working in London for over a decade. The partnership, formed in 2004, focuses on book design, illustration and visual identity work. In addition to their commissioned projects, they set up an online store in 2006 and have become renowned for their high-quality picture fonts and illustrations.

Andrzej Klimowski

klimowski.com

Born of Polish parents in London in 1949, Klimowski was trained at the Saint Martin's School of Art before studying at the Academy of Fine Art and working professionally in Warsaw. Klimowski's Eastern-European legacy deeply influences his work, which includes posters and book jackets, illustrations, TV graphics and animation. He is Professor in Illustration at the Royal College of Art, London.

Aleksandra Nina Knezevic

ninadesign.co.Bachelor's degree
ulupubih.com.Bachelor's degree

Aleksandra Nina Knezevic was born in 1973 in Sarajevo, Bosnia Herzegovina. She graduated from the Academy of Art's Graphic Design in Cetinje/Montenegro. Her works have been widely recognized and have received awards in Bosnia and Herzegovina and at Design Festivals worldwide, (Slovenia, Japan, England, Italy). She was art director of J.W.T. Studio – a marketing and advertising agency in Slovenia – and has also acted as illustrator for *Elle* magazine (Slovenia). Since 2006, she has been president of the Bosnian Association of applied artists and designers.

Nils Knoblich

nilsknoblich.com

Nils was born in 1984 in the small city of Stollberg, Erzgebirge, in Germany. He has been studying Visual Communication at the School of Arts and Design in Kassel since 2005. While drawing serious comics and illustrations, he also works on his own animation projects. In spring 2007 he completed his animated short film *1st Date*.

Jeff Knowles

mosjef.com

Jeff Knowles graduated with a Bachelor's degree (Hons) in graphic design from The University of Salford, and from there joined Research Studios London in 1998. During Knowles' time at RS he handled a variety of projects, from large branding projects, publication design, packaging design, motion graphics and web design. Knowles also has a keen interest in photography and has worked for studio projects including Segment Systems, The Royal Court Theatre and Somerset House. He also has a photography collection with Font Shop's fStop Images.

Koa Dzn

koadzn.com

Olivier Cramm, or Koa, is a Lille-based graphic designer and illustrator who founded design studio Koa Dzn. In 2005 Cramm joined forces with Parisian shop The Lazy Dog to publish *War of Monstars* – a postcard book featuring 80 colourful cards by 80 graphic designers and illustrators from around the world. The book's collaborative artworks feature Koa's monsters 'fighting' the creatures of his selected participants.

L

LAD
laddesign.net
supersonicsite.com
Lawrence Azerrad is an independent graphic designer and art director based in Los Angeles. Since 2001, Azerrad's studio LAD has produced work in film, print, digital media and album packaging. From 1996 to 2001 Azerrad worked at Warner Bros. Records as an art director and graphic designer. While at the record label, Lawrence created packaging and imaging for artists such as Elvis Costello, Miles Davis, Clint Eastwood, The Red Hot Chili Peppers, Brad Mehldau and Wilco. As an independent designer, clients include Virgin, IMF the International Music Feed, surf legend Laird Hamilton. Azerrad has continued designing for music, creating boxed sets and album covers for artists including The Foo Fighters, Philip Glass and Paul McCartney. He is an instructor in the Graphic Design department at Art Centre College of Design, and has taught Visual Literacy at The Academy of Art University, Graduate School of Graphic Design in San Francisco.

Elisabeth Lecourt
elisabethlecourt.com
Elisabeth Lecourt was born in France in 1972. She moved to the United Kingdom in 1992 and obtained her MA at London's Royal College of Art in 2001. Lecourt exhibits in Europe and the USA, and her work includes drawing, installations, paintings, embroidered handkerchiefs, sculptures and intricate dresses made from folded maps.

Less Rain, Tokyo
lessrain.com
Design agency Less Rain was founded 1997 in London, and has offices in Berlin and Tokyo. Co-founder Lars Eberle has been the creative director behind the majority of Less Rain's best work, and currently heads the Tokyo office.

Katharina Leuzinger
katleuzinger.com
Katharina was raised in Zurich by Swiss and Japanese parents. Her dual-nationality has influenced the style and structure of her artworks. She moved to London in 1996 to study Design at Central Saint Martins College of Art and Design and has since won various design awards from sources such as D&AD, Design Week and Creative Circle. She works across numerous media and is active in the UK, Europe and Australia.

Gastón Liberto
gastonliberto.blogspot.com
myspace.com/libertoarte
flickr.com/photos/reduccion
Gastón Liberto was born in Sierra Grande, Argentina. He studied Art and Philosophy in Rio IV, Argentina, where he and his classmates formed a circus that is still active. Since 2000 he has lived with his wife and muse Julieta Cerutti in Barcelona. His work is influenced by magic, realism and surrealist pop. He has been working in the fields of painting and sculpture for ten years.

Love to Post
lovetopost.co.uk
Love to Post (LTP) is a project by UK-based design student Martin Rimmer in which artists are invited to create artworks with blank postcards which are then displayed on the LTP website. The project is expanding to include international contributors and has received a lot of positive feedback. Rimmer himself hopes for a successful future in print and media advertising after his graduation.

Holger Lübbe
holgerluebbe.de
Holger Lübbe is a graphic designer and photographer. In 1999 he started his ongoing Give and Take project in South Africa while working on his Diploma in Communication Design at Fachhochschule Darmstadt, Germany. Give and Take has been adopted in other parts of the world, and pictures can be seen on Lübbe's website.

M

Marc&Anna
marcandanna.co.uk
London-based Marc&Anna is a graphic design consultancy founded by Marc Atkinson and Anna Ekelund. The consultancy focuses on creating work that communicates clearly and intelligently, with strong visual impact.

Garance Margot
garance.margot@free.fr
Garance Margot was born in 1969 in Switzerland. Following the acquisition of her Swiss Diploma, she studied illustration at the Arts Décoratifs de Strasbourg, France. Her work consists of painting and drawing directly onto photographic prints. Her main theme is the transformation of the human body. Garance has been living in Paris since 1996 and works as a freelance author, artist, graphic designer and illustrator.

Monokini
monokini.ch
Lausanne-based graphic design studio Monokini was founded by Nathalie Imhof and Marlène Jeannerat. Their clients include AVDC (Association Vaudoise de Dance Contemporaine, Lausanne), LUFF (Lausanne Underground Film & Music Festival), Musikvertrieb, Zürich and RSR – La Première, Couleur3, Option Musique, Lausanne.

Sofia Morais
sofiamorais.net
Lisbon-based graphic designer Sofia Morais graduated from the Fine Arts School of Lisbon. In 2003 she took part in the European Voluntary Service which gave her a chance to live and work in Spoleto, Italy. Sofia has since worked in a design studio in Lisbon which specializes in graphics and packaging design, and has also undertaken an Illustration course at the Gulbenkian Foundation.

Julian Morey Studio
abc-xyz.co.uk
eklektic.co.uk
London-based graphic designer and typographer Julian Morey worked for Peter Saville Associates, where he designed graphics for New Order, Factory Records and The Haçienda. Working independently for over ten years, his clients include Diesel Jeans, Environ Records, Arena, Asprey, The Body Shop, KesselsKramer, London Records, Pentagram, Royal Mail and *Vogue*. In 1999 he founded Club-21 as an outlet for his diverse collection of digital typefaces. Frequently profiled by the design press, these contemporary fonts have been incorporated into advertising for clients such as Nike and for stamps for the Dutch PTT. Morey also established the publishing company Editions Eklektic to showcase his more personal work in silkscreen prints and greetings cards.

Musa
musacollective.com
MusaCollective was formed in October 2003 by Raquel Viana, Paulo Lima and Ricardo Alexandre. In 2004 the Lisbon-based collective of graphic designers organized the MusaTour exhibition supporting the MusaBook project – the first Portuguese graphic design book ever compiled (published by idN Hong Kong). Projects such as *NLF Magazine*, the first Portuguese Qee 'Happy' toy and their exclusive, limited merchandizing goods (ThePack, HoleMug) followed. Commercial work developed by MusaWorkLab helped to put the Portuguese design scene firmly on the map.

My Brand Project
peter-wendy.com
Paris-based art director Xavier Encinas used to work freelance under the name of Rumbero Design before joining forces with Cécilia Michaud in 2007 to set up studio peter&wendy. The two had previously worked together, initiating and curating the 2004 collaborative My Brand Project – which featured works exploring the relationship between people and brands, by artists and designers from around the world.

Rick Myers
footprintsinthesnow.co.uk
Manchester-based Rick Myers' work is crafted using deceptively simple materials and processes – considering the countless interweaving elements, which include mobiles, hand-detailed prints, bitten work, wood diagrams, dust and paper sculpture. His acclaimed seven-year project, Funnel Vision Portable Museum was shown both at the 2004 Liverpool Biennial, and during British Architecture Week in Birmingham in 2005. He has collaborated on projects and publications with Nieves, 2K, Channel 4, Gladtree Press, Matt Krefting, Rebelski, Commonwealth Stacks, Hammer & Tongs, Voice of The Seven Woods and The Quiet Life, and has produced 100 artworks for CDs. Rick has presented exhibitions in Manchester, London, Germany, Sweden, USA and Japan.

N

Joana Niemeyer
joananiemeyer.com
Joana Niemeyer was born in Germany. She studied in Phoenix, Arizona and at the London College of Printing (now London College of Communication). In 2005 she obtained her MA in Communication Design from London's prestigious Central Saint Martins College of Art and Design. She now works with Thomas Manss & Company, in London.

NogoodCorp
nogoodcorp.com
Jordan Nogood is an artist and the founder of NogoodCorp. He lives and works in Woodland Hills, California, USA.

O

One Fine day
one-fine-day.co.uk
James Joyce is an artist and designer living and working in London. In 2006 he founded his own studio, One Fine Day, where he produces limited-edition prints of his work. He also undertakes commissions, and has worked for a wide range of clients, including Penguin books, Nike, *Creative Review*, Levi's, Kiehl's and Carhartt. Joyce has exhibited his work at The Flyer as Art in East London, RCA Secret at the Royal College of Art and, in March 2006, installed his work at the Carhartt flagship store in Covent Garden.

Osmotronic
matthewfalla.com
osmotronic.com
Matthew Falla is a London-based designer working in graphic and interactive design, employing media from print to motion graphics to conceptual interactive TV services and electronic devices. A graduate of the Royal College of Art in London, he is setting up a design consultancy, Osmotronic.

P

Danielle Palmstrom
danielle.palmstrom@gmail.com
Danielle Palmstrom graduated with a BFA in Graphic Design from Rhode Island School of Design (RISD) in 2006. She lives and works in New York City. Collecting found picture postcards, Palmstom screenprints silhouettes of herself onto the various antiquated settings of the cards.

Perception
perceptionnyc.com
Based in New York City and founded in 2001 by former award winning R/GA creatives Jeremy Lasky (design director), Brendan Werner (editorial director) and Daniel Gonzalez (effects director), Perception's mission is to create world-class commercial visual art that combines their clients' message with timeless design. Clients include CourtTV, Discovery Kids, SS+K, Brandbuzz, Sony, R/GA, AFG, Grey Worldwide, Sundance Channel, ABC, Bravo, Miramax, WE Channel, AMC, the entire ESPN family, Ogilvy and Mather, Playboy Entertainment, Grey Advertising, SportsNY, SpikeDDB, Time Warner, Showtime, Spike TV, Concept Farm and HBO.

Peskimo
peskimo.com
Peskimo is comprised of Jodie Davis and David Partington, who met at Leeds Metropolitan University before graduating in 2002 in Graphic Arts and Design and Multimedia Technology respectively. Their work is inspired by cartoons, vintage graphic design and the oddities of everyday life. They hope one day to own their own ice cream van.

Polite Cards
politecards.com
davidshrigley.com
Polite is an independent UK publishing company dedicated to creating original greeting cards, postcards and stationery. Cards feature the work of established artists such as Vic Reeves, David Shrigley and Bob and Roberta Smith. The latest addition to their range of artistic products is a box set of 25 postcards by David Shrigley – with a cover design produced by Shrigley specially for the project.

Georgina Potier
georginapotier.com
London-based freelance illustrator and designer Georgina Potier obtained her Bachelor's degree in Illustration at Kingston University in 2004 and subsequently her Master's degree in Communication Design at Central Saint Martins in 2007. Her clients include Random House, *Dazed and Confused*, Great Ormond Street Hospital, Project RED and Shift! among others.

R

Red Design
red-design.co.uk
Brighton-based Red Design was founded in 1996 by creative director Ed Templeton. Red has a reputation for creating award-winning graphic designs across a range of media, both in the UK and internationally. The company's success dates from 1997 when Mercury Records offered them a major label album campaign. In 1998 Red Design created the artwork for Fat Boy Slim's *You've Come a Long Way Baby*, which sold over seven million copies worldwide. Since then they have worked with most major and independent record labels. Clients include Penoyre and Prasad, MTV Europe, VIVA TV and Tanner Krolle.

Ben Reece
benreece.com
London-based Ben Reece studied Graphic Design at Parsons School of Design in New York and Illustration at London College of Printing and Universität der Künste in Berlin. Reece works both as a freelancer and for Neville Brody's Research Studios in London and Paris. Reece has worked on prints for Stella McCartney; moving image work for MTV, Channel 4 and the Tate Museum; created branding for the Barbican and Bonfire Snowboarding and Illustrations for Play Station and Kitty-Yo Records.

Rinzen
rinzen.com
Australian design and art collective Rinzen is known for the collaborative approach of its five members. With their 2001 book, *RMX*, they invited over 30 international participants to sequentially rework digital art, in what has now become a common method of collaboration among designers and illustrators. Rinzen's work embraces myriad styles and techniques, often featuring bold, geometric designs or intricate, hand-drawn studies. Rinzen's posters and album covers have been exhibited at the Louvre in Paris, and their large-scale artworks are installed in Tokyo's Zero Gate and Copenhagen's Hotel Fox. They designed the inaugural issue of Paul Pope's *Batman* for DC Comics and graphics for a bicycle released by Japanese company Bebike. Members of the group are based in Berlin, Brisbane, Melbourne and New York.

Alex Robbins
alexrobbins.co.uk
Alex Robbins is a freelance illustrator and graphic designer who graduated from Camberwell College of Arts, London. He has an experimental approach to image-making, using a variety of tools and skills with each project he undertakes. His work has been published in numerous books and magazines and his clients include *The New York Times*, *The Guardian*, *The New Yorker*, *Time Out*, Dunlop Shoes, Reader's Digest, Rojo and Macleans.

Royal College of Art
rca.ac.uk
London's Royal College of Art is the world's only postgraduate university of art and design, specializing in teaching and research and offering MA, MPhil and PhD degrees across the disciplines of fine art, applied art, design, communications and humanities.

S

S3
s3s3s3.com
S3 clients praise the company's combination of creativity, professionalism and responsiveness: *'As one of the few ISO 9001:2000 certified agencies in the United States, S3 is an efficient, accountable business partner: consistently on target, on time and on budget. S3 is also a WBENC-certified woman-owned business, providing diverse viewpoints and helping our clients achieve their diversity budget goals.'* S3 have offices in Boonton, New Jersey and Irvine, California.

Samia Saleem
samiasaleem.com
degreesnola.com
Samia Saleem received a Bachelors degree in Graphic Design from Loyola University of New Orleans in 2004. After Hurricane Katrina, she relocated to Seattle where she is back on track designing for web, motion- and print media. Following her experience with Katrina, she self-published *Degrees of Separation* – a postcard book containing the works of 24 graphic designers living in, from, or connected to New Orleans. Saleem's work has appeared in Beautiful Decay's Anthology, *Curvy (Design is Kinky)* and *Computer Arts Magazine* and has been featured as Macromedia's Site of the Day. Her work was nominated for a Webby Award.

Craig Salter
salter.cd@btopenworld.com
North Yorkshire-based Craig Salter studied Graphic Design at Leeds Metropolitan University. He gained experience at Exposure Design, in London before moving back up north to work at Wolseley and then Leeds-based Propaganda. He now works freelance in and around Yorkshire and the north of England.

Remco Schuurbiers
remcoschuurbiers.com
clubtransmediale.de
pingpongcountry.de
Remco Schuurbiers was born in the Netherlands and now lives and works in Berlin. His work includes abstract compositions, short video films, installations and live video performances. He collaborates with contemporary electronic musicians to produce composed or improvized audiovisual performances. Schuurbiers also works as a photographer, as one of the organizers of Club Transmediale and as co-organizer of the The Art of Pingpongcountry project. Together with director Ivan Stanev, he also creates films and theatre productions.

Set Editions
seteditions.com
Set Editions was founded in 2004 and is owned and designed by Alison Riley. The range of postcards and other cards are made of recycled and post-consumer materials – including foil-stamped postcards made from 100% recycled chipboard.

Andy Smith
asmithillustration.com
Andy Smith graduated from the Royal College of Art in London in 1998. Since then he has worked as an illustrator for clients such as Nike, Expedia, Mercedes, Vauxhall and Orange. As well as commercial work, he produces self-published books and silkscreen prints.

Studiobenben
benschlitter.com
geoandinfo.com
Ben Schlitter is an award-winning designer, illustrator and painter working mainly in acrylic and collage. Schlitter also works in illustration and designs print, interactive and motion graphic projects. His postcard set Geography and Information Distribution Project is designed to facilitate the distribution of geographical details. Studiobenben is based in Hays, Kansas.

Stoltze Design
stoltze.com
Boston-based Stoltze Design was founded in 1984 by Clifford Stoltze. The award-winning studio offers a wide range of strategic print, packaging and interactive design solutions. Clients include The American Institute of Graphic Arts, Boston Society of Architects, Boston Philharmonic, Capitol Records, EMI, Harvard University, Massachusetts College of Art, Matador Records, Rockport Publishers, Sony Music and the Society for Environmental Graphic Design.

Studio Output
studio-output.com
Founded in 2002, Nottingham's Studio Output specializes in design and art direction. Their multi-disciplinary approach has attracted clients such as Arts Council England, Ascot, BBC Radio 1, Coca-Cola, Channel 4, The Future Laboratory, USC, Ministry of Sound, Macaulay Sinclair, Puffin Books, Schuh, Shine Communications, The River and Walé Adeyemi. Their work has been featured in magazines and books around the world. The firm's partners are Rob Coke, Dan Moore and Ian Hambleton.

Stylorouge
stylorouge.co.uk
Stylorouge is an independent creative consultancy with over 25 years of experience in commercial media. Working in graphic design, art direction, advertising, film and television, photography and multimedia, they produce effective creative communication with originality and integrity for a variety of industries. Stylorouge specializes in the music business.

Sub Communications
subcommunication.com
subtitude.com
Based in Montreal, Canada, Sub Communications was founded in 1999 by Sébastien Théraulaz. Valérie Desrochers joined the studio in 2001. Sub is a young design studio whose commitment to high standards has made it a respected member of the graphic arts and new media community in Montreal. Sub is also responsible for the creation of Subtitude, a virtual environment dedicated to graphic experiment and the expression of new visual concepts.

Supermundane
supermundane.com
Supermundane is part of the new era of multi-disciplinary artists. With work published and exhibited worldwide, Supermundane was picked as one of 25 emerging design talents in 2004 by New York magazine *Step (Inside Design)*. Having exhibited in several solo graphic art shows, Supermundane has also produced work for Playstation, Orange, Hoegaarden, Colette, Juliet Lewis, Sleaze and Good for Nothing.

Kate Sutton
katesutton.co.uk
Since graduating from university, where she studied Graphic Arts, Kate Sutton has been working as a freelance illustrator. As well as taking part in multiple exhibitions, Sutton has worked with clients such as Howies, Roxy, Urban Outfitters and Nookart. Ornate patterns and carboot sales rank among the main influences in her work.

T

Tabas
tabas.fr
An arts and calligraphy enthusiast, Cédric Malo has been working as a graphic designer since 1996. In 2000 he set up his studio Tabas in Marseille, and has since carried out commissions for music labels and public institutions. His personal work – paintings on cardboard, photography and rag dolls – extends his craft-like approach. His colourful and playful designs are, by virtue of their simplicity, accessible to a large audience. Tabas is represented by Lezilus. His first monograph was published in 2004 as part of the design&designer series by French Pyramyd Editions.

Jo Taylor
thisisjo.com
London-based artist Jo Taylor makes postcards by hand-stitching texts onto envelopes with wool. Jo Taylor works with spoken and written English. Through slide and sound installations and stitching, she unearths and celebrates the patterns and complexity of language. She studied Fine Art at Edinburgh University and Communication Art and Design at the Royal College of Art.

Taxi Studio
taxistudio.co.uk
Taxi Studio was established in 2002 by Alex Bane, Spencer Buck and Ryan Wills. Whether they are busy designing packaging, logos or brochures, their aim is to achieve unique design results with tangible gains for their clients. Shell awarded them the Business of the Year title – one among the 70 creative awards they have been allocated. Taxi Studio is based in Bristol, UK.

Yorgo Tloupas
intersectionmagazine.com
yorgo.co.uk
Yorgo Tloupas is the co-founder and creative director of *Intersection* magazine. He commutes between his native Paris and London, where he works for the magazine, and as a freelance designer and art director for various fashion, art, music and automobile clients.

Toy2R
toy2r.com
With a passion to put toys in an art context, Hong Kong-based Toy2r is breaking down the barriers between product design, art and graphics. Founded in 1995, Toy2R is the first company to focus on the designer toy phenomenon, combining art and developing vinyl toys for the collectors market. The D.I.Y. Qee (pronounced *key*) figures begin as blank, three-dimensional canvases that artists subsequently design. The results materialize from the work of some of the biggest names in pop art and fashion, collectors and designers.

Rosanna Traina
rosietraina.blogspot.com
rosanna.traina@alumni.rca.ac.uk
London-based Rosanna Traina, image-maker and printmaker, obtained her Bachelor's degree in Fine Art (Painting and Printmaking) from Sheffield Hallam University in 1998. Later she studied at the Royal College of Art, in Communication Art & Design, where she received her Masters degree. Rosanna's focus is illustrative typefaces. Exhibitions include MAKE at the RCA (2007), Reproduced by Kind Permission (her solo show), at the Sumo Store and Gallery in Sheffield (2000), and Marks Out of Ten at the S1 Gallery in Sheffield (1999).

Claire Turner and George Hadley
claireturner79@yahoo.com
george@cdt-design.co.uk
Claire and George met at Kingston University while studying Graphic Design. Since then they've worked for several design companies in London. In 2006 they packed their bags for a year and travelled the world and created the collection A Year in Postcards during the course of their journey.

Twopoints.Net

twopoints.net

Martin Lorenz, founder of Twopoints.Net, has received several prizes and is frequently featured in international books and magazines. Born in Hanover, Germany, Lorenz moved to Darmstadt at the age of 18 to study Communication Design. Three years later he moved to the Netherlands, learned Dutch, and graduated from the Royal Academy of Arts in The Hague. Martin and his wife Lupi live and work in Barcelona, where they have founded a corporation specializing in strategic design and communication. The couple teach in design schools, lecture and also organize design workshops. Self-initiated projects since 2000 include *The One Weekend Book Series*, Chinese Whisper, Poster Series, Color Combinations and Cover Of The Week.

U

Un.titled

un.titled.co.uk

Un.titled are a multi-disciplinary creative agency. They enjoy long-term collaborative relationships with some of the world's largest and most influential brands. Un.titled's work is defined by its strong ideas and belief in the effectiveness of great design. Un.titled is based in Leicester, UK.

United States of the Art

unitedstatesoftheart.com

Hamburg-based Carsten Raffel, or Cargo and Jens Uwe Meyer or 'Jum', are United States of the Art (USofA) – which they describe as an ongoing project and virtual studio. Both founders studied Visual Communication in Germany, at Hildesheim and Bielefeld respectively.

V

Vaughan Oliver at v23

v-23.co.uk

Independent record label 4AD's identity was designed in 1980, and has been maintained by Vaughan Oliver and his collaborators for over 25 years. Supported by Chris Bigg since 1988, Oliver and Bigg's collaborative work is credited to studio 'v23' – the founding of which was the result of their creative partnership being formalized in 1998. Specializing in work for the music industry, their collaboration has attracted commissions for company identities, magazine design, books and book-cover design, special print projects, print advertising, and promotional campaigns and film direction. Clients include 4AD, V&A Publishing, L'Oreal, Central Saint Martins, Coco de Mer, Microsoft, Sony Playstation, Harrods, Alberto Aspesi, John Galliano and Young Vic Theatre. A highly successful retrospective of Vaughan Oliver's work in Nantes, France, in 1992 resulted in shows in Paris, Tokyo, Los Angeles, the UK and Athens. His work has been collected for the Victoria and Albert Museum archives and is on permanent exhibition in their Twentieth Century Gallery. *Vaughan Oliver: Visceral Pleasures*, a design monograph by Rick Poynor, was published in 2000 and *Vaughan Oliver and v23 Poster Designs* was published in 2005.

Vilderness

vilderness.com

katstubbings.com

Kat Stubbings is a London-based graphic designer and illustrator whose clients include Fold7, Orange Communications, Johnny Hardstaff studio, British Coffee Association, Mercado and her very own independent T-shirt label, Vilderness. Stubbings has also started to work with external screenprinting facilities who – with her careful supervision and direction – produce her T-shirts.

Studio for Virtual Typography

virtualtypography.com

Matthias Hillner was born in Germany where he trained first in photography, then in visual design. He received his Masters degree in Communication Art and Design at the Royal College of Art in 2001, and has subsequently worked for various London-based design agencies. Matthias returned to the RCA in 2004 to conduct a Master of Philosophy of Arts degree. His investigation into transitional typography led to the formation of the Studio for Virtual Typography, a design consultancy that specializes in developing typographic solutions for multi-media environments. The business development was supported by the NFTS (National Film and Television School), and sponsored by NESTA (National Endowment for Science, Technology and the Arts). Having worked as a sessional lecturer at Ravensbourne College of Design and Communication in Kent, and at the London Metropolitan University, Matthias was appointed course leader of Applied Graphics at Amersham and Wycombe University in Buckinghamshire in 2006. He also teaches typography at the University of Hertfordshire.

Visualdata

visualdata.org

Amsterdam-based designer Ronald Wisse creates flash-driven websites and architectural visualizations. His work has been published in *Play Loud!*, *Digit* magazine, *Xfuns Creative & Design* magazine, *Übersee 2*, *World-Widedesigners* (2007) and Taschen's *1000 Favourite Websites*. Other work includes websites for Maurer United Architects, DVD releases of TV series *24* and *Prison Break* and feature film *X-Men: The Last Stand*.

W

Christian Ward
christianward.co.uk
Christian Ward has been drawing for his entire life. He has developed his artistic fetishes for drawing mysterious femmes fatales, psychedelic mind clouds and men in capes trying to look dangerous. He is influenced by comic art and contemporary fine art as well as graffiti and graphics, art nouveau and film. Ward works in London, and favours sharp pencils, Promarker markers and Photoshop CS.

Frank Warren
postsecret.com
Small-business owner Frank Warren started PostSecret as a community art project. Since October 2004, Warren has received over 100,000 anonymous postcards, which have been featured in galleries, a travelling art exhibition, the popular music video for All-American Rejects' 'Dirty Little Secret' and in the bestselling *PostSecret* books. Ranked by *New York Magazine* as the third most popular blog on the internet, the website attracts over three million visitors a month. Frank has appeared on Today, 20/20, CNN, MSNBC, NPR and Fox News. He lives in Germantown, Maryland with his wife and daughter.

Simon Wild
simonwild.com
Cambridge School of Art graduate Simon Wild is a freelance illustrator. Inspired by travel and the collection of old toys that are kept in his studio, Wild creates illustrations that hint at a larger untold story. Simon has had his work featured in magazines, on music posters, album covers and projected on giant screens. He lives and works in Suffolk, England.

Jamie Wood
dubpixel.co.uk
London-based graphic designer Jamie Wood graduated from the Surrey Institute of Art and Design in 2005. He has been working on projects in the UK and abroad since leaving college. Wood is particularly interested in producing work which merges hand-drawn elements, found ephemera and vintage scraps into colour collage.

Stephen Woowat
woowat.com
dead-corps.com
Stephen Woowat graduated from Staffordshire University in 2005, after completing a three year course in Graphic Design. The postcard *Instant Mental Relief* that is featured in this book was the result of a final year project that was subsequently distributed by Boomerang Media, UK, in 2006. The original project was a winner at the 2005 Student Roses Awards, and earned Stephen a placement at Elmwood, Leeds, where he now works as a graphic designer on a variety of identity, branding and packaging briefs. Stephen pursues various independent design projects, including character creations for the fictional world of 'Dead Corps' – a grim corporation with an unusual workforce.

Y

Yee Ting Kuit
yeellustration.co.uk
Yee Ting is a UK-based freelance illustrator who graduated with first class honours from the Illustration degree course at University College Falmouth in 2006. Ting produces her work digitally using a combination of Photoshop, Illustrator and hand-drawn elements. Her work is influenced by bold colour, patterns, layers, texture, typography and printmaking techniques. Notable career highlights include being selected for the AOI's Images 31 exhibition in London, and commended in the YCN Design Awards 2007.

Yoki
yoki-lab.com
grouek.com
Born in 1976, Yoki is a graphic designer who lives and works in Paris. She creates illustrations mixing hand-drawn elements with photography. She is also art director at the Grouek web agency.

Z

Zeptonn
zeptonn.nl
Born in Arnheim, the Netherlands, in 1979, designer Jan Willem Wennekes is known by his alias, Stinger. Working as a freelance illustrator and graphic designer from his studio Zeptonn, in Groningen, he creates T-shirts, posters, logos, button badges, skateboards and books. Stinger's trademark artistic style fuses imaginative objects with analytical twists. Jan has worked with a number of organizations, including Threadless, Blik, Popcling, TeeTonic, SplitTheAtom, Cut it Out and Playstation.

FL@33
flat33.com
stereohype.com
bzzzpeek.com

FL@33 is a multi-disciplinary studio for visual communication based in London. Its founders Agathe Jacquillat (French from Paris) and Tomi Vollauschek (Austrian but from Frankfurt, Germany) studied at FH Darmstadt (Germany), Academy Julian, ESAG (Penninghen) (Paris), HDK (Gothenburg) and Camberwell College of Art (London), before they met on the Royal College of Art's post-graduate Communication Art and Design course in 1999. They set up their company in London in 2001. The studio's clients include MTV Networks, Sacla, BBC, Royal Festival Hall, Laurence King Publishing, Groupe Galeries Lafayette, Matelsom, Arts Affaires and Friends of the Earth. The two launched Stereohype.com – Graphic Art & Fashion Boutique in 2004, an international platform for both emerging and established talents. The duo have also released self-initiated projects such as the award-winning *Trans-form* magazine and online sound collection project bzzzpeek.com. FL@33 interviews, features and company profiles have been published online and in numerous magazines, newspapers and books around the world. Interviews featured on BBC Radio and NPR, America's National Public Radio, after *The New York Times*, along with its international supplements, featured an article about the bzzzpeek.com project. A FL@33 monograph was published in 2005 as part of the design&designer book series by French publisher Pyramyd Editions.

Agathe and Tomi have designed several books, including Laurence King's *200% Cotton: New T-shirt Graphics, 300% Cotton: More T-Shirt Graphics* and *Patterns: New Surface Design. Postcard* is the first major publication FL@33 have compiled, written, edited and designed.

If you would like to submit your own postcard art and design work for potential inclusion in future editions of this book, please visit our dedicated website at postcard-book.info

ACKNOWLEDGEMENTS

We would like to thank all of the people who responded to the call for entries for this book. We are very grateful for the number and quality of submissions we received, which far exceeded the number of pages available to us.

Special thanks must go to our publisher Laurence King and his team, especially Helen Evans, Gaynor Sermon, Felicity Awdry and Angus Hyland.

We would also like to thank all of the contributors who made their valuable time available to us, to point us in the direction of other people's work, assist with the By Invitation Only chapter, created or revised artworks especially for the book or prepared photoshoots for us.

Sincere thanks also to these particularly inspiring and helpful people: Vaughan Oliver and Chris Bigg, Michael Johnson, Dan Eatock, Frank Warren, Chris Knight, Cati Estrada, Andrzej Klimowski, Gavin Lucas, Erjon Malaj, Sue Bradburn and Martin Rimmer.

And, last but not least, we would like to thank our clients, collaborators and supporters, especially our families and friends.

2.24